D1472846

THE BASICS OF
MATTER

CORE CONCEPTS

THE BASICS OF
MATTER

JOHN O. E. CLARK

ROSEN
PUBLISHING®

New York

This edition published in 2015 by:

The Rosen Publishing Group, Inc.
29 East 21st Street
New York, NY 10010

Additional end matter copyright © 2015 by The Rosen Publishing Group, Inc.

Library of Congress Cataloging-in-Publication Data

Clark, John O. E.
The basics of matter/by John O. E. Clark.
        p. cm.—(Core concepts)
Includes bibliographic references and index.
ISBN 978-1-4777-7752-7 (library binding)
1. Matter—Juvenile literature. 2. Matter—Properties—Juvenile literature. I. Clark, John Owen Edward. II. Title.
QC173.16 C54 2015
530—d23

Manufactured in the United States of America

© 2004 Brown Bear Books Ltd.

CONTENTS

CHAPTER ONE

WHAT IS MATTER?

Everything in the world is made up of tiny particles. The smallest particles that can exist on their own are called atoms. Often, atoms join together to form slightly larger particles called molecules. All chemical compounds are made up of molecules.

There are just over 100 different chemical elements, each with its own kinds of atom. Most elements are metals, such as iron, copper, and aluminum. A piece of iron, for example, is made up of millions and millions of iron atoms. Some elements are gases, such as oxygen and hydrogen. Only two chemical elements are liquid at ordinary temperatures. They are the silvery liquid metal mercury and a poisonous reddish brown liquid that is called bromine.

The characteristics of substances formed when

A scanning probe microscope was used to create this image of the atoms that make up a piece of gold.

CHEMICAL BONDING

In ionic bonding one atom gives one or more electrons to another atom to form a chemical compound that consists of ions. Here sodium and chlorine combine to make sodium chloride. In covalent bonding the atoms share electrons. Here an oxygen atom shares electrons with two hydrogen atoms to form a molecule of water.

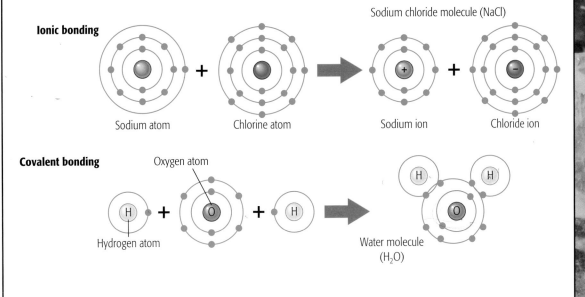

Sodium chloride molecule (NaCl)

Ionic bonding

Sodium atom   Chlorine atom   Sodium ion   Chloride ion

Covalent bonding   Oxygen atom

Hydrogen atom   Water molecule (H_2O)

DIFFERENT KINDS OF CARBON

The element carbon exists in two different forms. In graphite the atoms are linked in layers that slide easily over one another. Graphite is black and very soft. Diamond is another form of carbon in which the rigid structure forms the hardest crystals known.

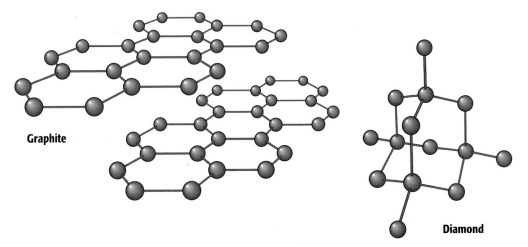

Graphite

Diamond

atoms of different elements combine are often very different from those of the individual elements. For instance, when the metal copper combines with the gas oxygen, it forms molecules of the nonmetal copper oxide. And the two gases hydrogen and oxygen combine to form the liquid we know as water.

ATOMIC STRUCTURE

Atoms are not solid balls of matter, like tiny plastic beads. They consist of a central core, or nucleus, surrounded by one or more electrons. Electrons are therefore even smaller than atoms. In fact, an electron is about one two-thousandth the size of the smallest atom. Also, electrons are electrically charged—each electron carries a single negative charge. The nucleus of the atom is also charged. Nuclei have a positive charge that balances the negative charges of the electrons. The

Carbon dioxide (CO_2)

Water (H_2O)

Methane (CH_4)

MOLECULE SHAPES

The shapes of molecules depend on how the atoms are joined to one another. In carbon dioxide the atoms join in a row, while in water they are joined at an angle. The hydrogen atoms in methane are arranged as a pyramid.

Table salt is made up of sodium chloride molecules.

electrons in an atom are arranged around the nucleus in layers called shells, rather like the layers inside an onion bulb.

The joining of atoms to form molecules involves the electrons. There are two chief ways that this can happen. Some kinds of atom—mainly metals—can lose one or more electrons. This leaves them with a positive charge, and such charged atoms are called ions. Other kinds of atom—mainly nonmetals—can gain one or more electrons. This gives them a negative charge, and they become negative ions. If a metal such as sodium reacts with a nonmetal such as chlorine, each sodium atom gives an electron to a chlorine atom. They have combined to form a molecule of sodium chloride, which is ordinary table salt. Sodium chloride consists of a mixture of sodium ions and chloride ions.

In another way of joining atoms the electrons do not move from one atom to the other. Instead, atoms share electrons. When hydrogen reacts with oxygen, they share electrons to form a molecule of water.

Water, made up of hydrogen and oxygen molecules, covers about 70 percent of Earth's surface.

CHAPTER TWO

GASES AND PRESSURE

Like all kinds of matter, a gas is made up of atoms or molecules. But these particles do not stand still. They rush around, bumping into one another and into the walls of their container. Collisions with the container create the pressure of the gas.

Gases make up one of the three states of matter—the other two are liquids and solids. We are surrounded by gas all the time because the air we breathe is a gas. In fact, air is a mixture of gases, mostly nitrogen and oxygen. You cannot

Helium is one of the two gases that are less dense than air—the other is hydrogen. Unlike hydrogen, helium does not burn. It is used to fill weather balloons and airships.

MEASURING GAS PRESSURE

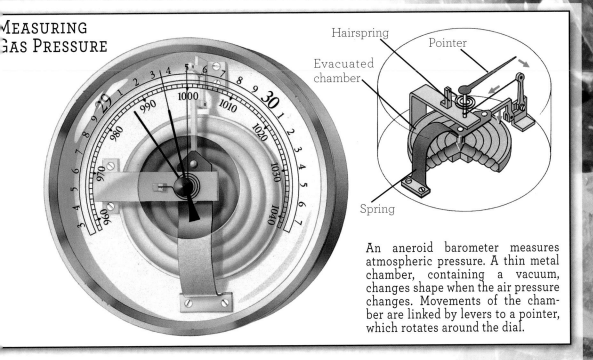

An aneroid barometer measures atmospheric pressure. A thin metal chamber, containing a vacuum, changes shape when the air pressure changes. Movements of the chamber are linked by levers to a pointer, which rotates around the dial.

see air, yet it has mass, and it exerts a pressure on everything that is in contact with it.

MEASURING AIR

The air in an average room weighs about 80 kg (about 175 lb). The weight of all the air in the atmosphere totals many millions of tons, and it presses on everything in it. At sea level this atmospheric pressure is about 1 kg on every square centimeter of surface (about 14 lb per sq in.).

The pressure of the atmosphere can be measured using a barometer. There are various kinds. The Italian scientist Evangelista Torricelli invented the first barometer in 1644. He took a long glass tube closed at one end and filled it with mercury. He then turned the tube upside down and lowered the open end into a bowl of mercury. The mercury did not all flow out of the tube. Its level fell slightly but then stopped, and the rest of the mercury remained in the tube. Torricelli reasoned that it was the pressure of the atmosphere pressing on the surface of the mercury in the bowl that held up the column of mercury. The space above the mercury in the closed end of the tube contained no air at all.

WEATHER AND PRESSURE

Normal atmospheric pressure will hold up a column of mercury about 76 cm (nearly 30 in.) tall. Because atmospheric pressure varies from day to day (because of the weather), the height of the mercury column also varies. People soon learned

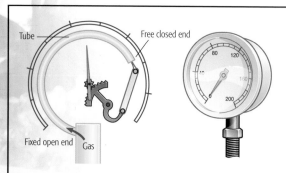

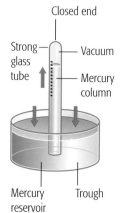

This type of pressure gauge is called a Bourdon gauge after its French inventor. It is based on a curved metal tube that is fixed at one end and free to move at the other. Gas under pressure enters at the fixed end and has the effect of slightly unbending the tube. This movement makes a pointer move around a dial.

A mercury barometer has a column of mercury that is closed at its upper end, with the open lower end in a trough of mercury. Atmospheric pressure pressing on the surface of the mercury in the trough supports the mercury column, whose length is a measure of the pressure.

Acetylene gas burns in oxygen with an extremely hot flame, which can be used for cutting or welding metal. This welder wears a mask to protect his eyes from the bright light of the torch.

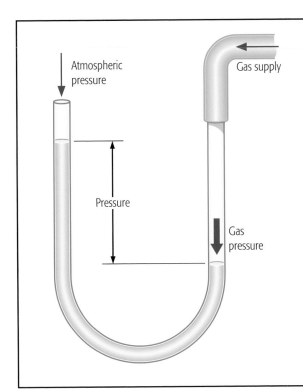

Atmospheric pressure

Gas supply

Pressure

Gas pressure

MERCURY MANOMETER

A simple device for measuring gas pressures is called a manometer. It consists of a U-shaped glass tube containing mercury. One end of the tube is open to the air, and the other end is connected to the gas supply. The pressure of the gas forces mercury up the open arm of the manometer. The difference in heights of the mercury columns is a measure of the pressure.

how to forecast the weather by watching the changes in pressure as revealed by a barometer. Clear, dry weather, for example, can usually be expected when the atmospheric pressure is on the increase. When the atmospheric pressure is falling, on the other hand, this generally indicates rainy weather.

Atmospheric pressure also decreases with height above the ground. It falls about 1 cm (about 0.4 in.) for every 100-meter (328-ft) increase in height. Barometers can therefore be used for measuring altitude. Many of the altimeters carried by aircraft are sensitive barometers. They are usually the aneroid type ("aneroid" comes from Greek words meaning "no liquid"). An aneroid

barometer does not contain mercury. The heart of the instrument is a closed chamber containing no air. As the external air pressure varies, the small vacuum chamber changes shape, operating a system of levers to move a pointer that indicates the value of the pressure on a dial. In an altimeter the dial is calibrated in height, not in pressure.

DENSITIES OF OTHER GASES

Not all gases are as dense as air. Two light gases are hydrogen and helium. Hydrogen is dangerously flammable. It was once used for filling balloons and airships, but it stopped being used after there were several disastrous fires.

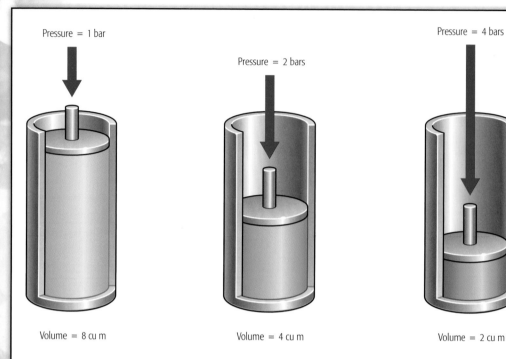

Pressure = 1 bar

Pressure = 2 bars

Pressure = 4 bars

Volume = 8 cu m

Volume = 4 cu m

Volume = 2 cu m

BOYLE'S LAW

The diagrams show the effect of increasing the pressure on a gas. When the pressure is increased from 1 bar to 2 bars, the volume is halved from 8 cu m to 4 cu m. Increasing the pressure to 4 bars reduces the volume to only 2 cu m. In other words, pressure is inversely proportional to volume. Put another way, the product of pressure and volume is constant.

Modern airships are filled with helium. This gas is less dense than air, which is why a helium-filled balloon or airship floats upward in the air.

Other gases are used as fuels. Methane occurs underground in natural gas. The similar gases ethane and butane are obtained from crude oil in an oil refinery. They are sold as bottled gas for heating and lighting in campers and trailers. The same gases are also known as LPG (liquefied petroleum gas) and are being used as a cleaner alternative to gasoline for automobile engines.

Acetylene is a fuel gas that is burned in oxygen in an oxyacetylene torch. The very hot flame is employed for welding and cutting steel and other metals. The acetylene gas is liquefied and supplied in steel cylinders. Carbon dioxide is a very dense gas. Nothing will burn in carbon dioxide, which is why it is used in fire extinguishers.

PRESSURE AND VOLUME

A gas in a closed container exerts a pressure. That is because the rapidly moving molecules of gas collide with the walls of the container. It is also why we have to keep the container closed—a gas will soon escape from an open container. If we decrease the volume of gas by making the container smaller, the pressure increases. For instance, the pressure doubles if we halve the size of the container. This relationship between gas pressure and volume was discovered by the British scientist Robert Boyle and for this reason is known as Boyle's law.

Heating a gas also increases the pressure as long as the volume is kept the same. That is because the hotter gas molecules move faster and collide with the walls more often. If the volume is not kept constant, heating a gas makes it expand and take up more room. An expanding gas can be made to do work, and several kinds of machine make use of this fact.

A flow of gas can also be made to do work. The earliest device that made use of moving gas was the sailing ship, where the moving gas is the wind. Later, people harnessed the wind with windmills. Many windmills had sails that resemble those on a sailing ship, and people in Mediterranean countries still make windmills like this.

ROBERT BOYLE

Robert Boyle was born in Munster, Ireland, in 1627, son of the Earl of Cork. He studied abroad in Switzerland before returning to England in 1644, settling in Oxford ten years later. He carried out many experiments in both physics and chemistry. Boyle investigated electricity, crystals, and relative density. He invented an air pump and studied the effects of pressure on gases. In 1662 he formulated Boyle's law: At constant temperature the pressure of a gas is inversely proportional to its volume. He later moved to London and became a founding member of the Royal Society. He was a great believer in finding practical uses for science. Boyle died in 1691.

CHAPTER THREE

ALL ABOUT LIQUIDS

Liquids are the "middle" state of matter. They are denser than gases, but not as dense as solids. And like gases, they flow readily and so have to be kept in a container.

The molecules that make up a liquid are free to move around. That is why a liquid has no definite shape—it just takes up the shape of its container. The container does not need a lid to prevent the liquid from escaping (unlike a gas). Also unlike a gas, a liquid cannot be compressed: increasing the pressure on a liquid does not make it occupy a smaller volume. But a liquid does exert a pressure on the sides and bottom of its container (and on anything that happens to be in it), and this pressure depends on the liquid's density and its depth. The greater the depth of a liquid, the greater the pressure.

Another property of a liquid is called viscosity, which is a measure of how thick it is. Machine oil and molasses are viscous

Water is the most common liquid on Earth. Here an aircraft drops tons of water on a fire in an attempt to put it out.

CAPILLARY ACTION

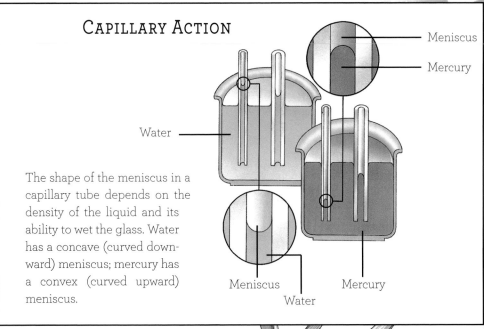

Meniscus

Mercury

Water

The shape of the meniscus in a capillary tube depends on the density of the liquid and its ability to wet the glass. Water has a concave (curved downward) meniscus; mercury has a convex (curved upward) meniscus.

Meniscus

Water

Mercury

A bug, such as a water boatman, is able to walk across the surface of a pond because of surface tension. The tension forms a "skin" on the surface that is strong enough to support the weight of the bug.

liquids, which flow only slowly. Water and alcohol are not viscous, and they flow easily. This is because the molecules in water, for instance, slide past one another much more easily than do the molecules in molasses.

SURFACE "SKIN"

The molecules at the surface of a liquid attract one another. This causes an effect, called surface tension, that makes the liquid behave as if it had an elastic "skin" on its surface. It makes it possible to float a needle on the surface of water in a glass and allows bugs such as pond skaters to walk across the surface of a pond. It is also why bubbles and liquid droplets are spherical.

A substance called a surfactant, also known as a wetting agent, can reduce surface tension. Detergents are surfactants, and adding them to washing water allows the water to get into small crevices in closely woven cloth and pry away any dirt that may be lodged there.

Another effect of surface tension is called capillary action, or capillarity. It is this effect that makes blotting paper or a sponge soak up water. It can be observed

A bubble's thin film of soapy water reflects light to create rainbows of colors.

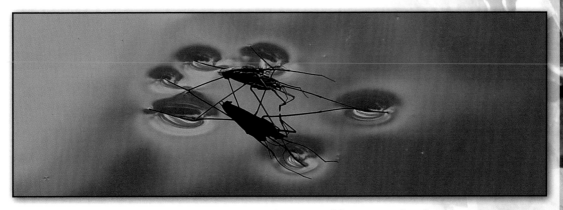

Insects called pond skaters, or water striders, are able to transfer their weight and run across the surface tension of water.

by lowering a narrow glass tube vertically into a liquid. With a liquid such as water, the liquid rises up the tube a little way. If you look closely at the surface of the liquid inside the tube, you will see that it is curved—it is higher at the sides of the tube than at the center. This curve, called a meniscus, is saucer-shaped in the case of water. But in a dense liquid such as mercury, the meniscus is curved upward—higher at the center than at the sides.

Surfactants, such as those in laundry detergents, are called "surface-active agents" because they can interact with two surfaces at once. They draw grime out of fabrics and keep it from getting back in.

CHAPTER FOUR

THE STRUCTURE OF SOLIDS

The atoms and molecules that make up solids are hardly able to move at all. They are held in a regular arrangement, which is responsible for the regular shapes of crystals.

Most solids are hard, rigid, and strong, and many have high melting points. All of these properties reflect the fact that their atoms are held together by strong interatomic forces. Some solids, however, consist of large

The expression "solid as a rock" is used to describe anything that is very solid. Dams are made of concrete, which is like artificial rock. It is solid enough to hold back the millions of tons of water in the lake behind it.

Diamond is among the most valuable of crystals. It is also the hardest solid known. These diamonds have been cut and polished for jewelry.

molecules that are held together by only weak intermolecular forces. They tend to be soft and have low melting points. Waxes and many polymers (plastics) are typical examples.

Crystals are solids in which the component atoms or molecules are arranged in a regular, repeating pattern called a lattice. When a crystalline solid is heated, its particles hold their positions in the lattice until the melting point is reached, when the solid suddenly melts. A solid that lacks this kind of regular internal arrangement of its particles is termed noncrystalline, or amorphous. Glass and plastics are amorphous solids. When they are heated, they soften gradually over a wide range of temperatures and have no definite melting point.

The exact nature of the particles in a crystal varies among different materials. In most metals and some other solid elements such as sulfur, or carbon in the form of diamond, the crystals are made up of atoms. In substances such as sugar, the crystal components are molecules. But in the vast majority of crystalline substances the particles are ions. Nearly all salts and minerals—and therefore rocks—are basically ionic solids.

PROPERTIES OF METALS

When we see the word "crystal," we tend to think of something clear and angular, like a sparkling diamond. Most metals are also made up of crystals. This fact, and the type of bonding between the particles within the crystals, explains most of the properties of metals.

A typical metal can be cut or polished to produce a shiny surface. Indeed, until people learned how to put a thin layer of silver on a sheet of glass, all mirrors were made of polished metal. Many metals can be drawn out so that the piece gets thinner and thinner to form wire. This property is called ductility, and we say that the metal is ductile. Many metals

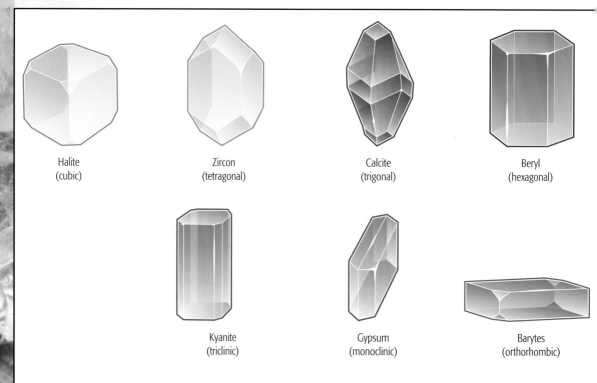

Halite
(cubic)

Zircon
(tetragonal)

Calcite
(trigonal)

Beryl
(hexagonal)

Kyanite
(triclinic)

Gypsum
(monoclinic)

Barytes
(orthorhombic)

CRYSTAL SYSTEMS

There are seven crystal systems, illustrated here by means of seven common minerals. The external shape is called the crystal habit. All crystals of the same substance always have the same angles between their faces. But the habit may vary because different faces may grow at different speeds.

can also be hammered into thin sheets. Gold, for example, can be beaten into gold leaf so thin that light passes through it. This property is called malleability, and we say that the metal is malleable.

Some metals, such as copper and gold, are both ductile and malleable. They have these properties because, when they are stretched or hammered, their atoms slip past one another so that the solid can take up its new shape. The kind of bonding in metals must therefore be different than that in other crystalline solids. In a metal the outermost electrons of the atoms easily become detached. This creates positive ions, which are surrounded by a "sea" of electrons. These electrons are free to move, and this accounts for the ability of a metal to conduct electricity. When a battery, for example, is connected across the ends of a piece of metal wire, the electrons flow along the wire and conduct an electric current. The free electrons also make metals good conductors of heat.

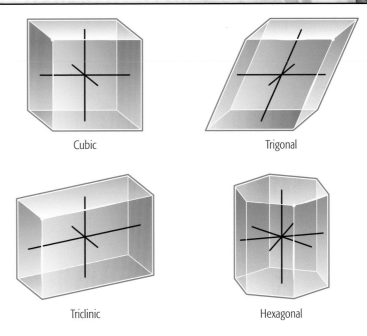

Cubic

Trigonal

Triclinic

Hexagonal

CRYSTALS AXES

The different crystal systems are defined in terms of imaginary axes drawn inside them. Six of the systems have three axes. The simplest is the cubic system, which has three equal axes at right angles. The hexagonal system has four axes.

SOLID BONDS

We have now identified four kinds of bonds that hold together the particles in solids. In substances such as diamond the atoms share electrons and are held together by covalent bonds (look again at the diagrams on page 7). In substances such as salt the particles take the form of positive and negative ions held together by electrical attraction called ionic bonds. In a wax the particles are molecules that are held together by intermolecular forces. And in a metal the atoms are held together by metallic bonds involving free electrons. But all four types of solid can form crystals.

BASIC CRYSTAL FORMS

To early scientists crystals presented a bewildering array of different forms. Natural mineral crystals come in all shapes, sizes, and colors. Gradually, the scientists realized that there are seven basic crystal forms, and all crystals belong to one of them. But natural crystals are seldom perfect and may become distorted while they slowly form in the ground, or they may be affected by the presence of impurities. Throughout the ages people have valued gemstones such as diamonds, emeralds, and rubies for their beauty and rarity. Even today, collectors eagerly seek perfect specimens of ordinary mineral crystals.

The seven crystal forms are called systems. Their names come from their geometrical shape. The simplest is the cube, which is represented in the cubic system. Common salt is found naturally as the mineral rock salt known to mineralogists as halite. It crystallizes as cubes. If you have a strong magnifying glass, you can use it to see the cubic shape of crystals of table salt.

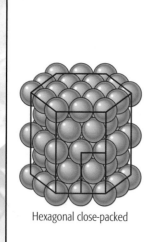

Hexagonal close-packed

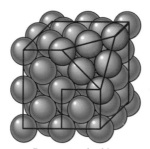

Face-centered cubic

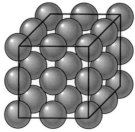

Body-centered cubic

Unit Cells of Crystals

The basic arrangement of atoms or ions in a crystal is called a unit cell. It determines the outward shape of the crystal. These three examples are common among metals and other crystalline substances.

Glass can be heated and softened and then formed into shapes.

UNDERSTANDING STRUCTURES

The particles within a crystal are arranged in a regular pattern called the crystal lattice. Common salt is composed of ions, and in the common salt crystal the ions are arranged at the corners of cubes. Salt crystals are also cubes, so in this case the shape of the crystal reflects the arrangement of ions in the crystal lattice. This is also true for many other crystal shapes. If you imagine eight ions at the corners of a cube, you can see that there is a space in the middle for another ion. This arrangement is the crystal lattice known as body-centered cubic. In another arrangement there is an extra ion at the center of each face of the cube. This pattern is called face-centered cubic.

In yet another arrangement there is a circle of six ions with a seventh ion in the middle. Picture arranging seven oranges in this fashion. Now imagine adding three more oranges on top of this layer. You could then add another layer of six, and so on, to build up what is called a hexagonal close-packed arrangement.

Scientists investigate the structure of crystals using X-rays. When X-rays pass through a crystal, the atoms or ions scatter the rays and the pattern of the scattered X-rays can be recorded on a piece of photographic film. Because of the regular arrangement of particles within the crystal, the scattered X-rays create a distinctive pattern of spots on the photograph. From this pattern the scientists can work out the crystal structure.

Rock candy, seen here, is made up of large sugar crystals. Food coloring is often added, too.

MAKE YOUR OWN CRYSTALS

When mineral crystals form underground, they do so as molten material or concentrated solutions that gradually cool. The slower they cool, the larger the crystals grow. You can grow your own crystals if you wish. First take a crystalline substance—sugar, salt, and alum work well. Then add the substance to a jar of warm water until no more of it will dissolve. Tie or fix one crystal to the end of a piece of thin thread, and suspend it in the solution (tie the thread to a pencil across the top of the jar). Set it aside for several days. Gradually, the crystal will get larger as the substance comes out of solution. The new solid follows exactly the same shape as the original crystal as the particles take their regular places in the crystal lattice.

These people are standing in a salt mine in Peru.

CHAPTER FIVE

WHY DO THINGS FLOAT?

Which is heavier, a piece of wood or a piece of steel? The answer depends on their sizes. A piece of wood the size of a table is heavier than a piece of steel the size of a pin. But a ton of wood weighs the same as a ton of steel.

A piece of steel may or may not be heavier than a piece of wood depending on their sizes. But steel is always denser than wood. The density of a substance is its mass divided by its volume. Steel has a density of about 7,800 kg per cu m (480 lb per cu ft), while the

A steel-hulled ship floats because it is hollow. It displaces its own weight of water. It rides higher in the water when it has no cargo and sinks deeper when it is fully loaded because then it weighs more.

density of wood is only about 700 kg per cu m (44 lb per cu ft), depending on the type of wood. So, on average steel is about 11 times as dense as wood.

Water has a density of 1,000 kg per cu m (62 lb per cu ft), higher than wood but much less than steel. That is why a piece of wood floats on water and a lump of steel sinks. Difference in densities is also why a balloon that is full of helium gas (density 0.18 kg per cu m) floats in air (density 1.3 kg per cu m).

For a piece of something to float, it must be less dense than the fluid—liquid or gas—it is floating in. Ice is less dense than water, which is why ice cubes float in a drink and icebergs float in the ocean. But ice is only a little less dense than seawater, which is why the greater part of an iceberg stays below the surface, often jutting out underwater and being a danger to ships that get too close.

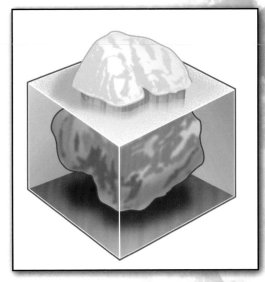

Icebergs float because ice is less dense than seawater. The density of ice is about nine-tenths the density of water. For this reason only 10 percent of the floating ice is above the water. The remaining 90 percent remains submerged.

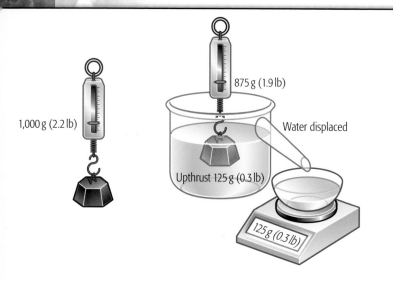

875 g (1.9 lb)

Water displaced

1,000 g (2.2 lb)

Upthrust 125 g (0.3 lb)

125 g (0.3 lb)

ARCHIMEDES' PRINCIPLE

When a weight is suspended in water, it appears to weigh less by an amount equal to the weight of water displaced.

Sometimes scientists use relative density instead of density. It is equal to the density of a substance divided by the density of water. It is a pure number with no units. Thus gold has a density of 19,000 kg per cu m (1,190 lb per cu ft) and a relative density of 19 (equal to the density of gold divided by the density of water).

COMPOSITE MATERIALS

Steel is a very strong metal alloy. Aluminum is not quite so strong, but it is much less dense (2,700 kg per cu m, or about 170 lb per cu ft). For this reason aluminum is used in space rockets and airplanes. A steel airplane would be three times as heavy as an aluminum one, and its engines would have to be three times as powerful to get it off the ground.

But some materials that have a low density are also strong. That is particularly true of composite materials, such as fiberglass and carbon fiber. Composite materials are made by combining two or more different materials to make a new material that is better in some way (usually stronger) than the ones it is made from. Fiberglass has thin hairlike strands of glass set in a plastic resin. It is slightly stronger than steel, but only one-fourth its density. It is used for making hulls for small boats, for fishing rods, and for the poles used by pole-vaulters. Carbon fiber is a similar material but is even stronger.

DISCOVERIES OF ARCHIMEDES

One of the oldest stories in physics is about a Greek mathematician and scientist called Archimedes, who lived more than 2,200 years ago. According to the story, he decided to take a bath and climbed into a tub that was full to the brim with water. Of course, as soon as he got in, the water overflowed onto the floor. But Archimedes was so pleased with what he had discovered that he ran out into the street crying "Eureka!" (which is Greek for "I have found it!").

What he had found was that an object immersed in water displaces its own volume of water. In addition, he also realized that the force keeping an object afloat—the so-called upthrust, or buoyant force—is equal to the weight of the water (or whatever fluid the object is floating in) it displaces. This last statement is known as Archimedes' principle. Any object that weighs more than the buoyant force will sink. But an object that weighs less than the buoyant force will float.

Another story about Archimedes shows how he put his principle to good use. Archimedes lived in the city of Syracuse on the island of Sicily. One day the King of Syracuse asked for his help. The king had been given a golden crown, and he asked Archimedes if he could find out whether it was made of pure gold (without melting down the crown and destroying it). Archimedes first weighed the crown and then immersed it in a bowl of water and measured the volume of water displaced. This volume of water equaled the volume of the crown. So Archimedes divided the weight of the crown by its volume, which gave him the density of the metal. He knew the density of pure gold, and so he could tell whether the crown was or was not made of pure gold. History does not record whether the crown was pure gold or not!

ARCHIMEDES

Archimedes was a Greek mathematician, engineer, and scientist who lived from about 287 to 212 B.C. He lived in Syracuse on the island of Sicily. In mathematics he found new methods of measuring areas and volumes, and he developed ways of dealing with very large numbers. He invented a pump that used a rotating, angled screw for lifting water, and he made pulley blocks for lifting very heavy weights. But he is best known for discovering Archimedes' principle, which states that the upward force on an object immersed in a liquid is equal to the weight of the liquid displaced. A Roman army attacked Syracuse in 215 B.C., and Archimedes was killed three years later by a Roman soldier.

DISPLACEMENT

Although steel is much denser than water, we can now begin to see how a steel ship floats. A solid lump of steel always sinks in water. But the hull of a steel boat is hollow. In water the hollow hull displaces an equal volume of water. The weight of water displaced equals the weight of the ship's hull, and so the ship floats. The weight of a ship is usually expressed as so many tons displacement, which is the weight of water it displaces. Some modern supertankers have displacements in excess of 500,000 tons. In a similar way airships displace their own volume when they "float" in the air. The air in a hot-air balloon is less dense than

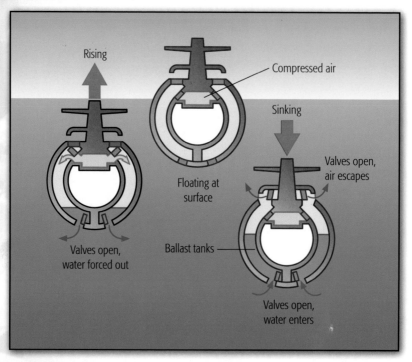

Rising

Compressed air

Sinking

Valves open,
air escapes

Floating at
surface

Valves open,
water forced out

Ballast tanks

Valves open,
water enters

A submarine sinks or rises in the water as its buoyancy changes. Letting water into the ballast tanks or forcing the water out with compressed air alters the buoyancy.

the surrounding air, which it displaces as it floats.

A submarine also has a hollow hull, but it is surrounded by tanks that can be flooded with water. On the surface the tanks are empty, and the submarine floats. To make it submerge, water is allowed into the tanks. The vessel loses buoyancy and slowly sinks. To surface again, compressed air is used to force the water out of the tanks. The vessel becomes buoyant again and rises in the water. The principle is the same for a small submersible and for a large nuclear submarine.

CHAPTER SIX

VAPOR AND STEAM

When a liquid is heated above a certain temperature, it boils. The liquid turns into a gas, usually known as a vapor. Steam is the gas or vapor formed when water boils. Liquids also turn to vapor when they evaporate, even though they are not boiling.

The molecules in a liquid are free to move around, allowing a liquid to flow and take up the shape of its container. When the liquid is heated the extra energy makes the molecules move faster and faster. They also move farther apart. Eventually, at a certain temperature called the boiling point, the molecules are so far apart that they become a gas. Usually the gas first forms within the liquid

An erupting hot spring, or geyser, is an impressive sight. Below the geyser groundwater flows down a channel in the rock, down to where the underground rocks are very hot. The heat boils the water, which forms steam. The pressure builds up until the steam explodes back up the channel, taking with it any water in its way.

near the base of the container that is being heated. The gas takes the form of bubbles, which move rapidly upward and make the liquid froth. Boiling is complete when the bubbles reach the surface and burst.

Different liquids boil at different temperatures. The boiling point of water, for example, is 100°C (212°F), while the boiling point of ether is only 34.5°C (94°F). That is so low that a drop of ether will boil if placed on the palm of your hand. The liquid metal mercury does not boil until it reaches a temperature of 358°C (about 676°F). That makes it a good liquid to use in thermometers. The metal tungsten, which is used to make electric lamp filaments, has the highest boiling point of all. It boils at the incredible temperature of 5,660°C (10,220°F), which is as high as the temperature at the surface of the Sun.

DIFFERENT BOILING POINTS

Various things can alter the boiling point of a liquid. A liquid boils when the pressure of the gas inside the bubbles is the same as atmospheric pressure—the pressure of the air at the surface of

the liquid. If we change the pressure, the boiling point changes. For instance, the air pressure at the top of a high mountain is much less than it is at sea level. As a result, water boils at a lower temperature at the mountaintop. For example, at an altitude of about 3,000 meters (about 10,000 ft) water boils at 90°C (194°F). Mountaineers say that it is very difficult to make a good cup of coffee at the top of a mountain—because the pressure is lower, the water does not get hot enough.

The 18th-century American scientist Benjamin Franklin once did a simple experiment that demonstrated the effect of pressure on boiling point. He heated water in a flask until the water boiled,

Here you can see bubbles of gas rising through water as it boils.

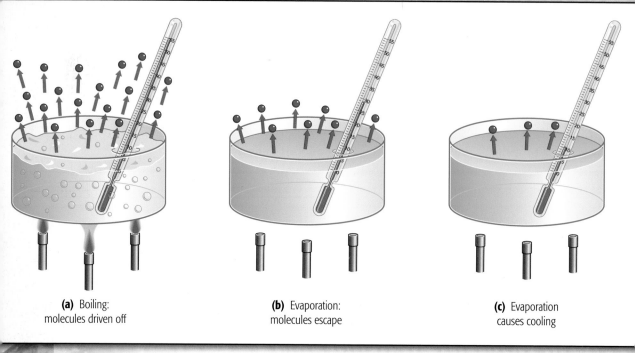

(a) Boiling:
molecules driven off

(b) Evaporation:
molecules escape

(c) Evaporation
causes cooling

In a boiling liquid (a) high-energy "hot" molecules leap out of the surface and form bubbles of vapor in the liquid. In evaporation (b) high-energy molecules leave the surface of the liquid even though it is not heated. As a result (c) heat energy is lost from the liquid, and it gets cooler.

then sealed the flask with a cork. The water soon cooled slightly, and boiling stopped. He then turned the flask upside down and poured cold water over it. Some of the steam above the water in the flask condensed, making the pressure inside the flask less than the atmospheric pressure outside it. As a result, the water started to boil again.

On the other hand, increasing the pressure on a liquid makes it boil at a higher temperature. This principle is used in an autoclave for sterilizing surgical instruments and in a pressure cooker for cooking food. If the pressure in the cooker rises to twice the atmospheric pressure, the boiling water is at a temperature of 120°C (248°F). As a result, the food cooks much quicker—potatoes cook in less than half the usual time. At 15 times the atmospheric pressure water does not boil until the temperature reaches 200°C (392°F).

The boiling point of a liquid also depends on its purity. An impure liquid boils at a higher temperature than a pure liquid. That is why adding salt

Wet laundry hung on a clothesline dries as the water evaporates.

to water raises its boiling point: potatoes cook quicker in boiling water with salt added. How much the boiling point rises depends on the concentration of the added substance. Chemists measure the rise in boiling point to find the concentration of a solution and can even use such measurements to calculate the molecular weight of the substance that is dissolved.

EVAPORATION

In boiling, heat makes a liquid turn to gas or vapor. But vapor can form without heat being applied. A puddle formed after it has rained gradually dries up. Where does the water go? It turns to vapor. We know that the molecules in a liquid move around. At the surface of the liquid some of the faster molecules leap right out of the surface, become vapor, and do not return. The name of this process is evaporation.

It can happen at any temperature but gets faster as the temperature rises.

The faster molecules leaving the surface during evaporation take heat energy with them. As a result, the liquid that remains gets cooler. That is why laundry hung out to dry gets cold as the water evaporates from it. And it accounts for the cooling effect of sweating. When a human or other animal sweats, the liquid perspiration evaporates, taking heat with it.

A simple device for keeping drinks cool works by the same principle. It consists of a porous pot, such as an unglazed flowerpot. It is soaked in water and placed over the drink, such as a carton of milk

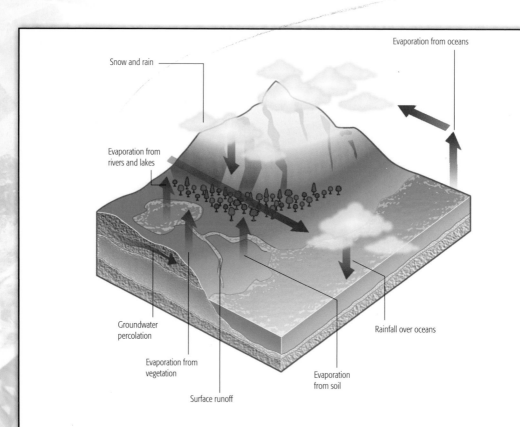

Snow and rain

Evaporation from oceans

Evaporation from rivers and lakes

Groundwater percolation

Evaporation from vegetation

Surface runoff

Evaporation from soil

Rainfall over oceans

THE WATER CYCLE

The water cycle describes how the Earth's water goes around and around, alternating mainly between the clouds and the oceans and rivers. In fact, 97.3 percent of the water is always in the oceans, with only 0.014 percent in lakes and rivers. Clouds account for even less—about 0.001 percent. Most of the remainder is locked up as ice in the north and south polar ice caps and in glaciers.

or a can of soda. As the water evaporates from the pot it removes heat and keeps the drink cool. Some wine bottle coolers work in the same way.

THE WATER CYCLE

Everyone knows that rainwater comes from clouds. But how did the rain get there? It all depends on the evaporation of water from rivers, lakes, and seas. It rises into the sky as water vapor, where it gets cooler and condenses into tiny droplets of water. The living processes of plants also give off water vapor, and that adds to the vapor in the sky. Clouds can be blown around by the wind, but eventually the water droplets get large enough to fall as rain. If it is cold enough, it falls as snow.

Melted snow and rainwater can go to various places. Most of it forms streams and rivers that eventually flow back to the sea. Some rainwater evaporates from the ground. Other water soaks into the ground and may reemerge in springs. And some of the groundwater is taken up by plants and passed back into the air from their leaves as water vapor. The whole circuit is called the water cycle.

The water droplets that make up clouds are big enough to scatter waves of light. The colors combine to give the clouds their white color.

CHAPTER SEVEN

MELTING POINTS OF SOLIDS

The molecules or atoms in a solid remain in a regular arrangement, which is what gives a solid its shape and hardness. At most, the particles vibrate slightly around their "fixed" positions. But what happens if we supply heat energy to a solid? It melts.

The effect of heat on a solid's molecules is to make them vibrate faster. Eventually they break away from their regular positions and move about freely, just as in a liquid. In fact, the solid has become a liquid—it has melted. Every pure solid undergoes this change at a definite temperature, called its melting point.

The melting points of different substances span a wide range of temperatures. Ice is a familiar solid—it is the solid form of water. It melts at 0°C (32°F), and its melting point is used as the lower fixed point on the Celsius temperature scale. The metal mercury, on the other hand, melts at –39°C (about –38°F). That is why mercury is liquid at ordinary temperatures. Tungsten melts at the very high temperature of 3,410°C (6,170°F). It is used to make the filaments of electric lightbulbs. In fact, there are very few things that will not melt if they are made hot enough—even rocks and concrete will eventually melt.

Here, a thick stream of molten lava flows down the side of a volcano in Hawaii. The rocks deep underground take the form of magma, which is kept liquid by intense heat and comes to the surface as lava when volcanoes erupt.

As pressure is applied to a snowball, some of the snow melts, then refreezes, creating a more solid ball of snow.

MELTING POINTS AND PRESSURE

We saw in the previous chapter how decreasing the pressure on a liquid lowers its boiling point. Pressure can also affect the melting point of a solid, although a lot of pressure is required to make much difference. The British physicist John Tyndall once devised a simple experiment to demonstrate this effect. He took a large block of ice (which is a solid) and supported it between two chairs. He then attached heavy weights to each end of a thin steel wire, and hung the wire around the ice block. The wire exerted a great pressure on the ice immediately under it, and the ice melted to form liquid water. The wire sank a little way into the water before the ice refroze above it. In this way, with alternate melting and freezing, the wire gradually cut its way right through the block of ice.

We make snowballs by taking a handful of snow and squeezing it. The pressure melts some of the snow, which refreezes

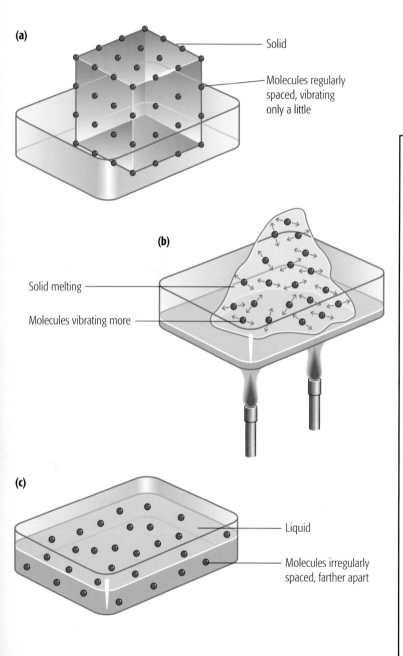

(a)

Solid

Molecules regularly spaced, vibrating only a little

(b)

Solid melting

Molecules vibrating more

(c)

Liquid

Molecules irregularly spaced, farther apart

MELTING MOLECULES

When a solid is heated, its molecules move faster and away from their regular positions in the solid. Order changes into disorder. Eventually the solid melts and becomes a liquid.

when the pressure is released, leaving a hard ball of snow. If the snow is too cold, we cannot squeeze hard enough to melt it, and it is difficult or impossible to make snowballs. Most solids expand on melting because their molecules are farther apart in the liquid state. This effect is put to good use in a device for automatically opening the windows in a room or greenhouse when the temperature rises to a certain point. The device consists of a cylinder of wax with a tight-fitting piston. As the temperature rises and the wax melts, it expands. This moves the piston, whose movement opens a window. The chemical naphthalene, sometimes used to make mothballs, also expands when it melts. A clever device for maintaining a constant temperature makes use of this property. A coil of wire

Greenhouses usually have plastic or glass roofs and walls. They trap heat from the Sun to maintain a warm temperature.

carrying an electric current inside a can of naphthalene gets warm and begins to melt the naphthalene. But as soon as it begins to melt, it expands. The expanding chemical presses a spring-loaded switch, which cuts off the electricity to the heating coil. So the naphthalene cools and solidifies again. The switch restores the current, and the action is repeated over and over.

CHAPTER EIGHT

COOLING AND FREEZING MATTER

Over the last few pages we have been looking at the effects of heat on liquids and solids. We did this by considering how heating changes the arrangement of atoms and molecules. In a similar way we will now look at the effects of cooling.

Heating a substance usually makes its atoms or molecules move faster. But cooling a substance has the opposite effect—it slows down the movement of atoms and molecules. When a gas is cooled, its molecules move more slowly and do not travel so far. This has the effect of reducing the pressure of the gas. If it is made even cooler, the molecules begin to behave like those in a liquid. The gas (or vapor) will have condensed into a liquid. That is what happens to the steam coming from the spout of a kettle of boiling water. In the cooler air the steam condenses to form tiny droplets of water. They are the white "steam" that we see; like clouds in the sky, it consists of water droplets. When we breathe out on a frosty day, the water vapor in our breath condenses into white clouds of water droplets. Real steam is invisible—and is dangerously hot because its temperature can be well over 100°C.

Clouds of steam rise above the cooling towers at a power plant. In fact, the clouds consists of tiny water droplets, like rain clouds. Actual steam—water vapor—is invisible.

As a gas cools, its volume decreases. In fact, at constant pressure all gases "shrink" by 1/273 of their volume at 0°C for every degree Celsius fall in temperature. For instance, if a gas is cooled from 0°C through –137°C, its volume is halved. This relationship between the volume of a gas and temperature is called Charles's law, after Jacques Charles, the French scientist who discovered it. It is usually stated in this form: The volume of a fixed mass of gas at constant pressure is proportional to its absolute temperature. Absolute temperature is Celsius temperature plus 273, so you can see where the fraction 1/273 comes from.

USING LIQUEFIED GASES

If the pressure on a gas is increased sufficiently, it turns into a liquid. Or at least this is true of many gases. There are some, however, that have to be cooled as well as being put under pressure before they will liquefy. The temperature below which they must be cooled is called the critical temperature. For example, carbon dioxide gas cannot be liquefied by pressure alone unless it is cooled below 31.3°C (88.3°F), which is its critical temperature.

Some gases have to be made extremely cold indeed to liquefy them. At ordinary pressure oxygen liquefies at –183°C (–297.4°F), and liquid nitrogen forms at –195.8°C (–320.2°F). Liquid air also has a temperature of about –196°C (–321°F). Such liquefied gases have various uses in science and industry, particularly where low temperatures are required. For example, a ship's propeller has to be an extremely tight fit on the propeller shaft. To get the propeller on, liquid air is first poured over the shaft to cool it. This makes the shaft shrink slightly so that the propeller can be slid on. When the shaft warms up, it expands and locks immovably into the propeller.

Other liquefied gases, such as liquid helium (which is the coldest), are used to surround and cool large computer

COOLING SEQUENCE

The effect of cooling on the states of matter is illustrated here. Cool a gas sufficiently, and it condenses into a liquid. Cool a liquid, and it eventually freezes to form a solid.

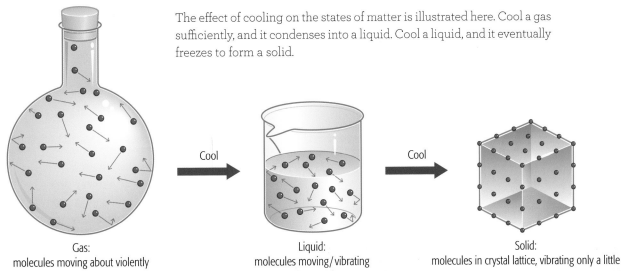

Gas:
molecules moving about violently

Cool

Liquid:
molecules moving/vibrating

Cool

Solid:
molecules in crystal lattice, vibrating only a little

memories and also big magnets used in medical scanning machines. Liquid air is also used as a source of other gases that occur naturally in air, such as neon, used in advertising signs. Liquid hydrogen is used as a rocket fuel, and liquid nitrogen is employed as a refrigerant and for liquefying natural gas.

FROM LIQUID TO SOLID

If cooling a gas turns it into a liquid, cooling a liquid turns it into a solid. The temperature at which this occurs is called the freezing point of the liquid. It is exactly the same as the melting point of the solid. At the molecular level the molecules of a liquid move less and less as they cool down until they take up the ordered arrangement of the solid. Water

droplets in a cloud, for example, turn into six-sided snow crystals on cooling. Water in bulk turns to ice. Sometimes you can cool a liquid below its melting point without it freezing. This is called supercooling.

If the temperature of the supercooled liquid rises slightly, the solid and liquid forms exist together for a while until the whole lot solidifies. A supercooled liquid is unstable. Stirring it, adding a speck of dust, or introducing a crystal of the solid substance will all make it turn into a solid.

Another type of supercooling occurs with glass. Glass is an amorphous solid—that is, it has no crystalline structure. Fusing together sand, lime, and soda (sodium carbonate) makes common, or soda, glass. This is a transparent substance, although it may be slightly colored by impurities. When liquid glass cools, it solidifies and can be used to make hundreds of everyday objects, including bottles, jars, and windows. But there is some evidence that glass never really "forgets" that it was a liquid. In the windows of very old European churches the glass may be significantly thicker at the bottom of the pane than at the top. Some people believe that over the centuries the glass has flowed, like a very, very thick liquid, and become thicker at the bottom.

These cars are driving on an icy road. Adding salt to ice makes the ice melt, because salt water freezes at a lower temperature than pure water. But unless plenty of salt is used, the salty water freezes again.

UNUSUAL PROPERTIES

As a liquid cools, it slowly crystallizes to form a solid. The nature of the crystals depends on how fast the liquid cools. If it cools rapidly, only small crystals have time to form. But if the liquid cools very slowly, there is time for large crystals to grow. These effects are best seen with minerals, large crystals of which form only if cooling has been slow.

But even when a solid has been formed, its properties can be affected by further cooling. Ice is a very unusual solid in this respect. Most solids shrink in size as they get colder. But ice actually expands, by as much as 10 percent. This can have disastrous effects on water pipes and the engine blocks of automobiles, which may burst if the water in them freezes. But it does mean that ice is less dense than water, which is why it floats. This is important for fish and other aquatic creatures in winter. Ice forms as a layer on the surface of a pond or river, so the fish remain unfrozen in the warmer water beneath.

Metals may also have unusual properties at low temperatures. The crystal structure of some metals changes. The crystals grow larger, and the metal loses strength, becoming brittle and snapping easily. At very low temperatures, close to absolute zero, some metals lose their electrical resistance. There seems to be nothing to stem the flow of electricity through them, and they become what are called superconductors. Researchers continue to search for materials that are superconductors at higher temperatures.

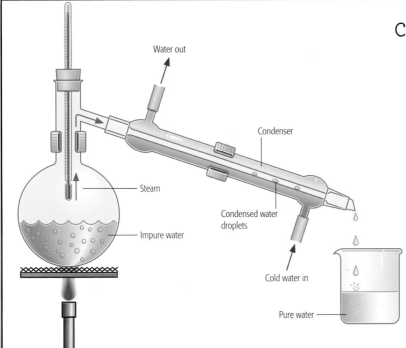

Water out

Condenser

Steam

Condensed water droplets

Impure water

Cold water in

Pure water

CHEMICAL CONDENSER

This apparatus is used in chemistry laboratories to condense vapors into liquids. Here it is being used to purify water. The impure water is boiled, and the steam produced (containing no impurities) is condensed to make pure water. The apparatus was invented by the German chemist Justus von Liebig and is called a Liebig condenser in his honor.

CHAPTER NINE

PUTTING GASES TO WORK

Compressing a gas requires an input of energy. The resulting compressed gas is therefore a store of energy that is capable of doing work. Scientists and engineers have devised many ways of using the energy of gases under pressure.

I t is important to remember that, scientifically, a vapor is a gas. Common vapors include steam and the mixture of gasoline and air that provides the source of energy in an automobile engine.

AIR COMPRESSORS

To make use of compressed gases, we must either compress them where we use them or store the gases under pressure for use somewhere else. The gas that is most commonly employed in the latter way is compressed air. It is produced by a machine called—not surprisingly—a compressor. Most compressors consist of an engine or a motor that works a piston.

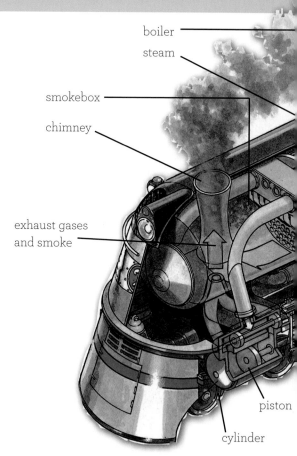

boiler
steam
smokebox
chimney
exhaust gases and smoke
piston
cylinder

The tender, pulled behind the locomotive, carries a supply of water and fuel—in this case fuel oil. The hot gases produced by burning oil in the firebox pass along tubes inside the boiler. The water surrounding these firetubes boils and produces steam. The steam is led to the cylinders before being vented up the chimney. This makes a draft, which pulls hot gases and smoke through the boiler's firetubes. Connecting rods and cranks make the back-and-forth movement of the pistons turn the driving wheels.

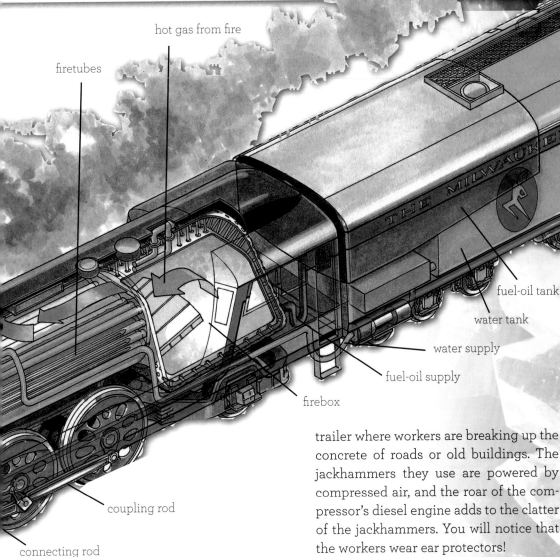

firetubes

hot gas from fire

fuel-oil tank

water tank

water supply

fuel-oil supply

firebox

coupling rod

connecting rod

The piston moves rapidly back and forth in a cylinder to compress air, which is stored in a strong metal tank or in cast-iron bottles called cylinders.

Cylinders of compressed air have many uses, from blowing up balloons for a party to working a spray gun for repainting an automobile. You may have seen a large portable compressor on a trailer where workers are breaking up the concrete of roads or old buildings. The jackhammers they use are powered by compressed air, and the roar of the compressor's diesel engine adds to the clatter of the jackhammers. You will notice that the workers wear ear protectors!

Another type of compressor has a rotary motion and works a bit like a water pump. The fastest types are equipped with blades like the blades of a turbine. Every jet engine has a compressor like this to compress the air for burning the vaporized fuel in the engine. Again, it is a noisy arrangement, and much of the din of a jet engine comes from the whine of the compressor.

STEAM-ENGINE PISTON

In a double-acting steam engine steam first enters one side of the piston and pushes it (a) before valves divert steam to the other side of the piston to push it back (b).

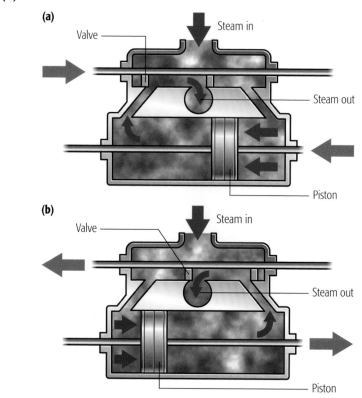

(a)

Valve

Steam in

Steam out

Piston

(b)

Valve

Steam in

Steam out

Piston

BIRTH OF THE STEAM ENGINE

The first machine to really exploit gas pressure was the steam engine. Invented in the 18th century, the first machines made use of the pressure of the air. Steam entered a cylinder and was condensed by a spray of cold water. This left a partial vacuum in the cylinder, and atmospheric pressure then pushed down a piston. These machines were therefore known as atmospheric engines. Soon the Scottish engineer James Watt started building engines that used the pressure of steam to move the piston, and that remained the basic principle of all steam engines.

Steam engines introduced the Industrial Revolution. Stationary steam engines drove spinning machines and looms in textile factories, and portable engines on wheels were employed for

SIMPLE AIR COMPRESSOR

A bicycle pump is an air compressor. When the handle is pulled back (a), air moves past the piston into the barrel. When the handle is pushed in (b), the piston fits tightly and compresses the air.

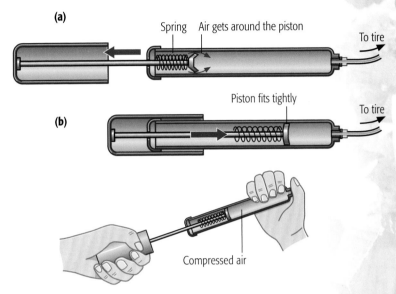

(a)

Spring   Air gets around the piston

To tire

Piston fits tightly

(b)

To tire

Compressed air

plowing. Steam engines powered boats, road carriages, and eventually locomotives for railroads. From about 1830 to 1930, steam power was the main type of traction on the world's railroads. Steam locomotives are still in service in India, China, and Russia.

The key parts of a steam locomotive are a fire, which heats a boiler for making steam, and a cylinder mechanism that uses steam pressure to produce motion. The fuel for the fire may be wood, coal, or oil. The heat from the fire passes along tubes that run the length of the boiler and are surrounded by water. The boiler is therefore called a firetube boiler. The steam, now under high pressure, moves

a piston back and forth in the cylinders (see the illustration on page 50). Systems of valves open and close to let the steam into the cylinders, and out again when it has done its work. The waste steam passes up a chimney, along with the smoke from the fire.

INTERNAL COMBUSTION

In a steam engine the fuel is burned outside the engine itself—it is an external combustion engine. Toward the end of the 19th century inventors in Germany and elsewhere began to make engines that burned fuel inside them—they were internal combustion engines. The earliest type

A jackhammer is powered by compressed air. The air is released in rapid bursts, causing a piston to hit the top end of the cutting chisel. A French engineer invented the jackhammer in 1861 for drilling into rock to make the first tunnel through the Alps between France and Italy.

used flammable gas, such as coal gas, and later a mixture of gasoline and air, as fuel. It was exploded inside the cylinders of the engine, and the rapidly expanding hot gas moved the pistons within the cylinders. An electric spark from a spark plug ignited the gasoline vapor. This is still the principle on which most of the world's automobile engines work.

The German engineer Rudolf Diesel invented another type of internal combustion engine. But in the diesel engine, as it came to be called, the compression of the vaporized fuel is enough to make it explode—there is no need for spark plugs. From its way of working it is also known as a compression–ignition engine. Diesel engines are now commonly used in trucks, some railroad locomotives, and increasingly, automobiles.

There is a third type of internal combustion engine that has no pistons at all. It uses the hot gases from burning fuel to turn the blades of a turbine and for this reason is called a gas-turbine engine. The blades of a compressor are mounted on the same shaft as the turbine blades. It is located in front of the turbine, and its job is to compress air for feeding into the combustion chamber. When they are first started, these engines need an electric motor to spin the shaft and get the compressor working before fuel is injected and ignited. A jet of hot gases leaves the rear of the engine, giving it its more common name—the jet engine. There are various types, used to power both military and civil aircraft.

Gas-turbine engines power some modern high-speed railroad locomotives. They are also used in small power plants (to drive electricity generators) and as standby engines in large power plants for use in the event of a steam-turbine breakdown.

CREATING PUSH

Similar in some ways to jet engines are rocket engines. They too burn fuel in a combustion chamber, and the resulting hot gases expand through a nozzle at the rear and create the thrust to push the rocket along.

But it is not the jet of hot gases pushing against the air that creates the thrust of a rocket engine. It is the reaction force against the front of the combustion chamber that gives the forward "push." For this reason, rocket engines are known scientifically as reaction motors.

All the internal combustion engines just described—and steam engines—use the oxygen in the air to burn their fuel. A rocket is different because it carries its own oxygen supply. A liquid-fueled rocket, such as the giant Saturn V employed to launch the American Apollo Moon shots, has tanks of liquid oxygen and liquid hydrogen as fuel. Solid-fueled rockets, as their name suggests, burn a solid fuel. The simplest of them burns gunpowder, like the rockets used as fireworks. It takes time to prepare a liquid-fueled rocket for launching, but solid-fueled rockets are ready to use right away. They power military missiles and act as launch boosters for larger rockets. And because they have their own supply of oxygen, all rockets work in the airless conditions of outer space.

Explosives that push shells and bullets out of the barrel of a gun are similar to solid rocket fuel. The firing pin of the gun detonates a small charge in the base of the cartridge, which in turn explodes the main charge. The large volumes of hot expanding gases produced push the bullet rapidly out of the barrel.

CHAPTER TEN

PUTTING LIQUIDS TO WORK

Unlike gases, liquids cannot be compressed. This means that pressure applied at one place in a liquid is transmitted immediately to every other part of it. This important principle is used in hydraulic machinery, from large presses for stamping out automobile bodies to bulldozers and backhoes.

The molecules in a gas are relatively far apart. When we apply pressure to a gas, the molecules are squeezed closer together, and the volume of gas gets smaller. But the molecules in a liquid cannot be squeezed any closer together. As a result, a liquid cannot be compressed. Applying pressure can, however, move a liquid. This is what a pump does. The pump on a fire truck forces water along the hoses with enough pressure to produce a jet of water that can reach the roof of a building.

MEASURING PRESSURE

Pressure is a force acting over an area. It is equal to the total force divided by the area concerned. The scientific unit of pressure is the pascal, named after a French physicist who

The water in a firefighter's hose has to be at high pressure. A pump in the fire truck provides the pressure.

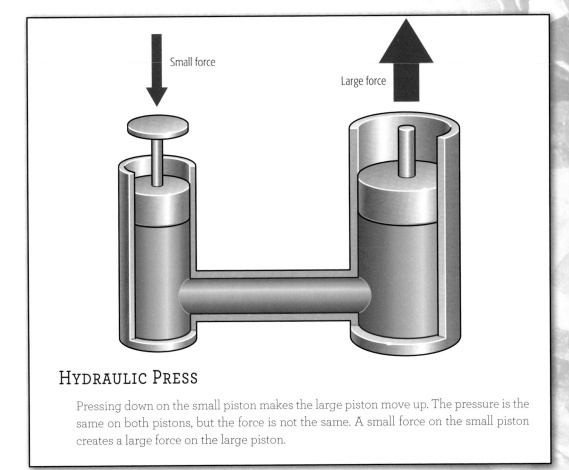

Small force

Large force

HYDRAULIC PRESS

Pressing down on the small piston makes the large piston move up. The pressure is the same on both pistons, but the force is not the same. A small force on the small piston creates a large force on the large piston.

studied the subject. In customary units pressure is usually given in lb per sq in. (which is sometimes abbreviated to psi). A single lb per sq in. is equal to nearly 7,000 pascals.

There are various other pressure units. The millibar is used in weather forecasting to express the pressure of the atmosphere. One millibar equals 100 pascals. The word "atmosphere" is also the name for a unit of pressure. It is equal to the average pressure of the Earth's atmosphere at sea level and is about 100,000 pascals or 14.7 lb per sq in.

SMALL PRESSURE, BIG PRESSURE

A hydraulic press has two pistons: a small one and a large one, connected by a pipe (see diagram above). The arrangement is filled with an oily liquid. Because pressure is transmitted equally throughout a liquid, a small force on the small piston results in a greater force on the large piston. For example, if the large piston has ten times the area of the small piston, a weight of 1 kg (2.2 lb) placed on the small piston will raise a weight of 10 kg (22 lb) placed on the large piston.

However, the large piston will move up only a tenth as far as the small piston moves down. For this reason, a practical hydraulic press has an arrangement of valves that allow the small piston to be pumped down repeatedly to raise a heavy weight. A common application is in the braking system of automobiles and trucks. When the driver presses on the brake pedal, it pushes a piston in what is called a master cylinder. Pipes connect this cylinder with slave cylinders at each wheel. Hydraulic fluid in the pipes transmits the pressure to the slaves, where the movement of their pistons applies the brakes. Because of the magnifying effect of using small and large cylinders, a fairly small force from the driver's foot creates a large force to apply the brakes. Many other machines make use of hydraulic pressure, such as dump trucks, bulldozers, and even large airplanes, which employ hydraulics to work the undercarriage and wing flaps. Most of them do not rely on the movement of a piston in a small cylinder to create the fluid pressure. Instead, they use rotary pumps to pressurize the hydraulic fluid, which is routed by a system of valves.

Hydraulic Backhoe

All the movements of the backhoe arm and bucket are produced by hydraulics. Notice the piston-and-cylinder arrangement at each of the pivots. A pump pressurizes the fluid inside the pistons and in the pipework connecting them.

CHAPTER ELEVEN

MOVING THROUGH FLUIDS

We have seen on earlier pages many of the differences between gases and liquids. But in some respects they can be alike, and scientists then use the single word "fluid" to stand for both gases and liquids. Here we look at flowing fluids.

The great white shark's body is perfectly streamlined so that it moves through the water effortlessly. The water nearest the shark's body moves along with it. As a result, the tiny striped pilot fish can swim along with the shark without getting left behind.

Many engineers need to know about the way things move through fluids. A speedboat slicing through the water, a jet plane flying through the air, and a supersonic bullet speeding to its target all have to be designed to push their way through a fluid. But it is difficult to study objects moving through fluids. Instead, engineers usually observe the fluid flowing past the object. The results are much the same.

All surfaces that make contact with each other experience friction, and objects moving in fluids are no exception. Friction opposes the movement, so it has the effect of slowing down a moving object. It also generates heat. A bullet is very hot when it reaches its target, and the surface of a meteorite burns away through friction when it arrives from space and plunges into the Earth's atmosphere at many kilometers per second.

One way of reducing the effect of friction on fast-moving objects is to design their shape so that friction is reduced to a minimum. A rifle bullet is the best shape for the job. Round bullets or square ones would not travel straight through the air—they would tumble about and probably miss their target. A normal bullet shape is streamlined, and streamlining accounts for the shapes of ship's hulls and high-speed airplanes. In the natural world many fish (such as sharks) and birds (such as swallows) also have a streamlined shape.

STREAMLINING AND TURBULENCE

Streamlines are the paths followed by all the particles of a fluid as they pass a particular point. It is as if the fluid consists of parallel layers—in fact, streamlined flow is also called laminar flow (from the Latin word for "layer"). The fluid as a whole keeps on moving smoothly in the same direction.

If an object moving in a fluid (or around which a fluid is flowing) does not have a streamlined shape, eddies and whirls begin to form in the fluid. This is called

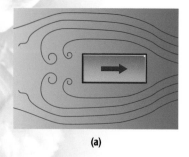
(a)

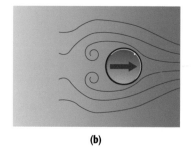
(b)

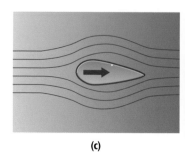
(c)

MOVING THROUGH FLUID

When a rectangular block moves through a fluid (a), it creates much turbulence. A sphere (b) is better, but the best shape of all is a teardrop (c).

The streamlined shape of an airplane helps it move through the air with as little resistance as possible.

turbulent flow. It can be seen, for example, in the water at the foot of a waterfall.

Turbulence can also affect fluids flowing through pipes. That is why pipelines are made smooth on the inside with no obstructions or sharp bends. In this way the fluid flows as quickly as possible. The rate of flow equals the speed of the fluid multiplied by the cross-sectional area of the pipe. If the speed cannot be kept as fast as possible, the only way to increase the rate of flow is to make the pipe wider, and that is often a very expensive option.

PRESSURE AND FLOW

If a pipe includes a section that is narrower than the rest, the speed of flow is obviously affected. The speed increases in the narrow part, to maintain the same overall rate of flow through the whole pipe. At the same time, the pressure of the fluid falls in the narrow part. The actual pressure change can be calculated using a complicated mathematical expression called Bernoulli's equation, which also takes into account the fluid's density.

The equation makes some useful predictions about fluid pressure. It tells us that the pressure in a fluid depends on its depth. That is why a dam is built of thicker concrete near the bottom, where the pressure of water behind it is greatest. Pressure also increases with depth in the sea, for example, which is why the hulls of submarines have to be made very strong. If not, they would be crushed by the pressure.

A simple experiment demonstrates this effect. Take an empty plastic drink bottle (2-liter or quart size), and make three or four holes, one above the other, down one side. Put a single strip of tape over all of the holes, and fill the bottle with water. Place the bottle in the sink and pull off the sticky tape. The water will jet out of the holes, but which stream goes farthest? It is the one near the bottom of the bottle, where the pressure is the greatest.

There are a number of practical applications of Bernoulli's equation, which predicts that a reduction in pressure of a flowing fluid causes an increase in the speed of flow. In a chemist's Bunsen burner or in a plumber's blowtorch, for example, gas passes through a small jet before it burns at the end of a tube. This speeds up the flow of gas and lowers the pressure, which sucks in air through the holes in the sleeve around the end of the tube. The air mixes with the gas and produces a much hotter flame than if the gas burned on its own.

AIRPLANES AND LIFT

It takes force to push an object through a fluid—jet airliners need very powerful engines. The resistance to movement is called drag, and streamlining is one way of keeping drag as low as possible. But how does an airplane fly in the first place? The answer has to do with the design of the wings.

An airplane wing is not flat. It is slightly curved in section, with more curvature on the upper surface than on the lower surface (see the diagram at the top of the opposite page). This shape is called an airfoil. As the wing moves through the air, the airflow is diverted. Some passes under the airfoil, and some flows across the upper surface. The air flowing over the top of the wing has slightly farther to go, so it has to speed up. As a result, the air pressure falls slightly (as is predicted by Bernoulli's equation). So, the air pressure is higher beneath the wing than above it. This provides an upward force called lift, and lift is what keeps the plane in the air.

To achieve maximum lift, the whole wing is angled upward slightly. The steeper the angle, the more lift is generated. But that is true only up to a point: If the wing is angled too much, the airflow ceases to be streamlined. Turbulence sets in above and behind the wing. At too steep an angle there is no lift at all—the airplane stalls, and unless the pilot takes action to prevent it, the plane will fall out of the sky.

USING MODELS

Ship's hulls, cars, and airplanes are all streamlined to reduce drag and thereby improve efficiency. Having to overcome drag wastes fuel. So engineers use models to test streamlining (which is very much less expensive than building a supertanker or supersonic plane to find out!). Models of ship's hulls are tested in a long narrow tank of water called a ship tank. Models of cars and planes are tested in a wind tunnel. The model is kept stationary, and air is blown past it at high speed by large fans. Smoke may be introduced into the airflow to highlight the streamlines around the model.

Airfoil Surfaces

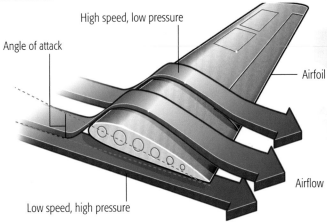

High speed, low pressure

Angle of attack

Airfoil

Airflow

Low speed, high pressure

The airfoil that forms an airplane's wing is slightly more curved over the top than beneath. This results in a pressure difference as the wing moves through the air, producing lift.

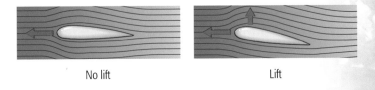

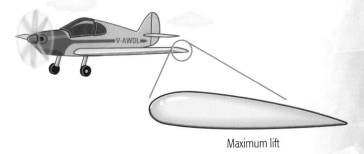

Maximum lift

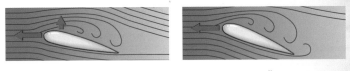

No lift

Lift

Less lift

Stall

The amount of lift depends on the angle of the wing to the horizontal. If it is angled too steeply, turbulence sets in and can result in stall, with no lift at all.

CHAPTER TWELVE

COMPRESSION AND TENSION

Solids can resist deforming forces much better than gases and liquids can. But there is a limit even to the strength of solids—if you strain them enough, they will break. For lower strains they will return to their normal shape when the strain is removed.

Two key properties of most solids are strength and hardness. Nowhere are these properties used to better effect than in the construction industry. Over the ages the chief permanent materials for construction have been stone, brick, concrete, and steel. They can be compared by considering how builders and engineers

This three-tiered arch bridge is a Roman aqueduct. It was built of stone across a valley in France.

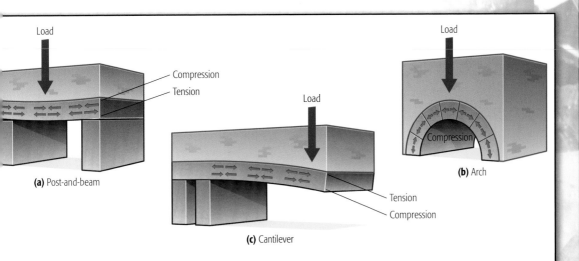

Load

Compression
Tension

(a) Post-and-beam

Load

Tension
Compression

(c) Cantilever

Load

Compression

(b) Arch

BRIDGE CONSTRUCTION

The three main kinds of bridges differ in the way compressive forces are set up. The decks of the post-and-beam (a) and cantilever (c) are also under tension.

have solved the problem of building over a space to make a bridge.

The earliest material for bridges, not counting tree trunks and vines, was stone. The simplest stone bridge consists of a single slab across two supports, called a post-and-beam construction. But the length of such a span is limited to the longest piece of stone available. Masonry—square-cut pieces of stone—and its artificial imitator, brick, were next to be used. And the secret of using these materials for spans is the arch. Many of the arches built in ancient Egypt, Greece, and Rome are still standing today.

An arch is a sturdy structure because the materials making it are strong in compression—that is, when they are

being squeezed. Each stone in an arch is in compression, and together they carry the load to the arch supports. Concrete also has good compressive strength. But reinforced concrete, which has steel rods within its structure, is also strong in tension (when it is being stretched). A cantilever bridge is built into supports at each end. When it is loaded, a cantilever beam is in tension on the top and under compression beneath. Reinforced concrete is a good material for making bridges in this way.

Steel is also strong in both tension and compression, and can be used for all types of construction. There is a practical limit to the length of a steel girder, but this limitation is overcome by making

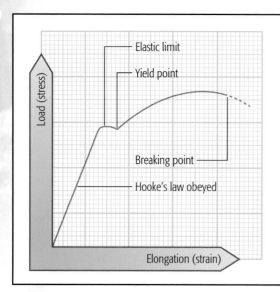

Elastic limit

Yield point

Load (stress)

Breaking point

Hooke's law obeyed

Elongation (strain)

HOOKE'S LAW

As a metal sample is stretched, the load (stress) is proportional to the elongation (strain) up to the elastic limit. This is Hooke's law. Beyond the yield point the sample stretches rapidly until it snaps at the breaking point.

trusses. Several short girders are joined together to make a rigid structure formed of triangles. Trusses are also much lighter in weight than any solid construction.

ELASTICITY AND BREAKING POINT

One property of steel and most other metals is elasticity. Scientifically, an elastic material is one that stretches under tension but returns to its original length when the tension is released. This property is very obvious with rubber and some plastics, which are collectively known as elastomers. But metals are also elastic, up to a point. That point is called the yield point. Imagine adding weights to the end of a length of wire fixed to a support at its upper end. As more weights are added, the wire stretches. If the weights are removed, the wire returns to its original length. In fact, the stress on the wire (the

weight) is proportional to the strain (the amount it stretches). This relationship is known as Hooke's law, after the English scientist Robert Hooke, who discovered it in 1678.

If we keep on adding weights to the end of the wire, a point will be reached—called the elastic limit—where the wire does not return to its original length. It is permanently stretched. Beyond the elastic limit, at the yield point, the wire continues to stretch with very little extra load until it finally breaks.

WIRES AT WORK

A metal that is ductile can be pulled out to form wire. That is usually done in stages by pulling the wire through a series of dies. Each die is slightly smaller than the previous one, and the wire gradually gets thinner.

Wire has many uses, particularly as a conductor of electricity. But wire is also used in construction. Several strands of wire can be twisted together to make a cable. Such cables are stronger than a single strand of the same thickness. Their most spectacular use is in suspension bridges, in which two or more long cables hang in an arc between two towers. Other thinner cables hang down from them to support a deck, which may be a roadway or a railroad.

MIXING METALS

As well as their density, most metals are also known for their hardness. This property results from the tight packing of the atoms in the crystals that form metals. Soft metals, such as aluminum and iron, can be made hard by alloying them with other elements, which modifies their crystal structure. Aluminum is mixed with magnesium or copper, and iron is alloyed with carbon to produce steel.

KINDS OF STRESS

The three main kinds of stress are compression, when a material is squeezed; tension, when it is stretched; and shear, when the top and bottom are pulled in opposite directions.

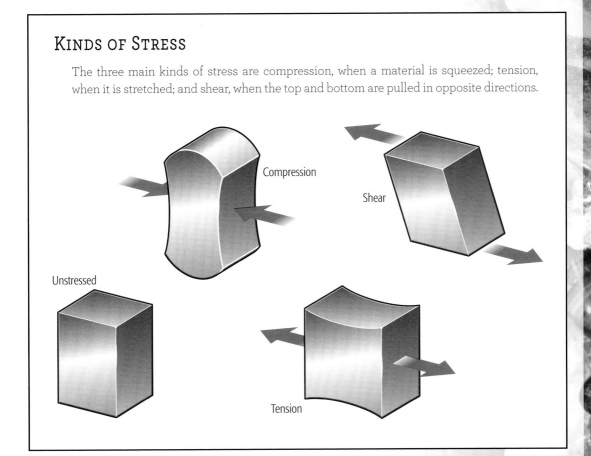

Compression

Shear

Unstressed

Tension

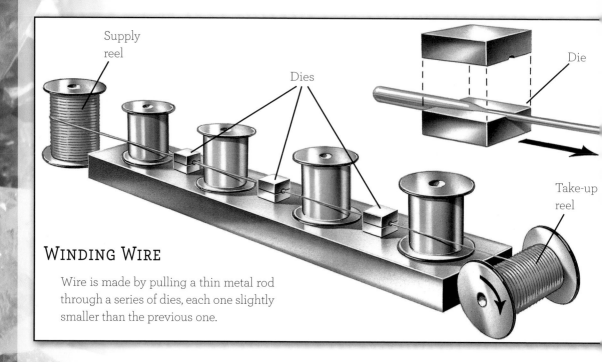

Supply reel

Dies

Die

Take-up reel

WINDING WIRE

Wire is made by pulling a thin metal rod through a series of dies, each one slightly smaller than the previous one.

Steel is created by combining iron and carbon. Nickel, titanium, and other elements are sometimes added as well to create alloy steel.

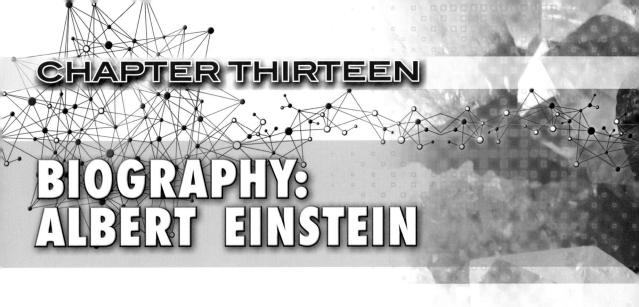

CHAPTER THIRTEEN

BIOGRAPHY: ALBERT EINSTEIN

The greatest scientist since the English mathematicican, physicist, and astronomer Isaac Newton (1642–1727) and the best known of the 20th century, Albert Einstein began work in a patent office. In 1905 he published his special theory of relativity; it was followed in 1915 by his general theory of relativity. Both revolutionized physics. Within 40 years, Einstein's theories had been put into practice in the development of atomic bombs and nuclear reactors.

Albert Einstein had an unsettled childhood. He was born in Ulm, Germany, on March 14, 1879, the son of a Jewish businessman, Hermann Einstein, whose business ventures forced the family to keep moving. In 1880 they went to Munich, where Hermann and his brother Jakob set up an electrical engineering business. When the enterprise ran into difficulties, the family left Germany for Italy, but Albert remained in Munich to complete his schooling. He was not a particularly gifted pupil, but his uncles Jakob and Cäsar encouraged

Einstein's theories are a major part of modern physics.

KEY DATES

1879	March 14, born at Ulm, Germany
1896	Renounces German citizenship
1896-1900	Studies at the Federal Polytechnic School, Zurich
1901	Acquires Swiss citizenship
1902	Begins work at the Swiss Patent Office, Bern
1903	Marries fellow-student Mileva Maric
1905	Publishes special theory of relativity
1909	Appointed associate professor at the Universty of Zurich
1911	Appointed professor of physics at the University of Prague
1914	Serves as director of theoretical physics at the Kaiser Wilhelm Institue, Berlin
1915	Publishes general theory of relativity
1933	Leaves Germany for the United States and takes a post at the Institute for Advanced Studies, Princeton, New Jersey
1940	Becomes a US citizen
1955	April 18, dies in Princeton, New Jersey

his interest in mathematics and science. He joined his family in Italy in 1894, and later moved to Switzerland.

Although there was as yet no sign of the genius he was to become, as a child Einstein showed an unusual curiosity. According to one story, at the age of five his father gave him a small pocket compass. Einstein was fascinated by the way the needle always pointed north. "There had to be something behind the objects, something that was hidden," he recalled thinking. At the age of 12 he came across what he later described as his "sacred little geometry book." This was a geometry text called *Elements*, by the Greek mathematician Euclid (around 300 BC). Einstein claimed that it presented a "clarity and certainty, which made an indescribable impression on me." In 1896 he began studying at the Federal Polytechnic School in Zurich, Switzerland. Einstein had an independent approach to learning and read the works of great 19th-century physicists instead of attending lectures. Although he graduated in 1900, he failed to secure a university post. Instead, after some searching around, he gained a post as an examiner at the Bern Patent Office.

ANNUS MIRABILIS

The year 1905 is best known as Einstein's "annus mirabilis," Latin for "wonder year." The same term has been used for 1666 in

RELATIVE TIME

Einstein's special theory of relativity argued that events that seem to happen at the same time are not necessarily experienced at the same time by different people. He gave the following example. Observer A is in the middle of a train, which is moving uniformly. Two bolts of lightning strike the ground at C and D, equidistant from A. Observer B who is standing at the side of the track directly opposite A, sees both bolts hit the ground at the same time. But observer A, who is moving toward D, will see D before C because the light from D will have a shorter distance to travel to A. Thus for A, events C and D do not happen at the same time.

The argument that there is no "absolute" time is the source of the "twins paradox." One 21-year-old twin stays on Earth while the other goes off in a spaceship. Say the spaceship travels at 95 percent of the speed of light for 15 years. The nearer the speed of light an object travels, the more its length decreases, and its mass increases. An effect of this would be that time measured on a clock on board would pass more slowly; in the time it took to record 20 minutes on an Earth-based clock, the spaceship clock would record one hour. So while 15 years pass on Earth, only five years go by on the spaceship. On return to Earth the astronaut would be 26 years old (21 + 5) but his twin would be age 36 (21 + 15).

relation to Isaac Newton: it was in 1666 that Newton developed his theory of gravity, gave his account of the nature of light and color, and also laid the foundations of calculus in mathematics. But whereas Newton's work mostly consisted of notebook entries, sketches of planned work, and other unpublished ideas, Einstein's accomplishment included fully worked-out theories, and five scientific papers, all of which were actually published in 1905. Nobody has ever matched this achievement. It is also unusual because the theories and papers were not compiled by an academic, but by an unknown physicist working in an office.

QUANTA AND UNCERTAINTY

Two key ideas developed in physics at about the time Einstein was working on his revolutionary ideas: quantum theory and the uncertainty principle. Both theories were advanced by German scientists. The first was put forward in about 1900 by Max Planck (1858–1947), and the second some time later, in 1927, by 26-year-old Werner Heisenberg (1901–1976).

Planck trained as a physicist in Munich and Berlin. After two university posts he joined the teaching staff at the Friedrich-Wilhelm (later Humboldt) University of Berlin in 1889, where he remained for 37 years until he retired. Planck's revolutionary insight was gained when he began considering how a hot object radiates energy (heat and light). The process can be seen as we watch a black object being heated; it passes through colors from red-hot, through orange, and up to white-hot.

Planck knew that light moves in waves, and that different colors correspond to different wavelengths. Red has the longest wavelength of visible light, orange has a shorter wavelength, and so on. So as the black object is heated, it is radiating energy of a range of different wavelengths; the hotter it gets, the more light with shorter wavelengths it is giving out.

However, observation contradicted classical theory, which stated that any hot object should be emitting energy in a burst of light of the same, short wavelength; in other words, that it should always be the same color. The only way Planck could find to explain why this was not the case was by supposing that its energy is not emitted continuously in waves, but as separate "packets" with specific frequencies. It was as if a car could increase its speed from 59 mph to 61 mph without ever traveling, for however brief a moment, at exactly 60 mph.

Planck called these individual packets quanta (singular, quantum), from the Latin word for "how much?" He also suggested that the higher the frequency of the waves, the greater the energy of each quantum was, and that beyond certain high frequencies the emission of a quantum would require more energy than could be provided, so the rate of radiation from the object would be reduced. This explained why a hot object does not emit its energy in the way that classical theory predicts.

Planck had introduced quantum theory, which operates beyond the limits of the classical physics of Isaac Newton and his followers. Einstein used quantum theory in 1905 to explain the photoelectric effect. In 1913 Danish physicist Niels Bohr (1885–1962) used it to explain the structure of atoms. The importance of Planck's theory was recognized in 1918 when he was awarded the Nobel Prize in Physics.

In classical physics, and indeed in normal life, we tend to assume that we can measure, at least in principle, the position and speed of any object. But in 1927 Heisenberg, then working with Niels Bohr in Denmark, argued that at the quantum level this cannot be done. In the quantum realm moving particles do not have both a precise position and a precise velocity at the same time. In fact, Heisenberg argued, the more we know the position of a moving particle, the more its velocity becomes uncertain, and vice versa. The phenomenon is called the uncertainty principle, and it is linked to the dual wave–particle nature of light. Although people often imagine that the "uncertainty" is to do with our inability to measure tiny particles accurately enough, this is not the case; it is a basic feature of the universe. Einstein had helped lay the foundations of quantum theory in 1905, but did not agree with some of its developments. Much of his own later work was spent trying to show that Heisenberg was wrong; however, he was not able to disprove Heisenberg's theory, and nor has anyone since.

CORREO

MAX PLANCK
1858 - 1947

Max Planck's work changed the way scientists studied physics.

QUANTA AND PHOTONS

Scientists at the end of the 19th century believed that for light, electricity, and magnetic forces to travel through space, they must be carried in a medium known as the ether. No one had been able to prove the existence of the ether, but there seemed to be no other explanation. Scottish physicist James Clerk Maxwell (1831–1879) had shown the connection between magnetism and electricity and demonstrated that electromagnetism was radiated in waves. Wavelength is the distance between successive crests or troughs, and frequency, the number of crests passing a particular point each second. Clerk Maxwell also showed that light is a form of electromagnetic wave. The second of Einstein's 1905 papers concerned the photoelectric effect, which is the way that some metals eject electrons (elementary particles) when light shines on them. Following Clerk Maxwell's wave picture, light was thought to behave very much like the waves of the sea as they crash on the shore. As the waves break and fall, they may move lines of pebbles up and down the beach. But the force of the waves is not strong enough to propel individual pebbles into the air.

Yet this is what seemed to happen with the photoelectric effect, a phenomenon first described by German physicist Philip Lenard (1862–1947) in 1899. He noted that when light fell on a metal surface, individual electrons (negatively charged particles) were thrown off, and that their velocity seemed to be related to the color of the light. Blue light, for example, produced more energetic electrons than red light. Increasing the intensity of the light seemed to have no effect on the velocity of the released electrons. The electrons produced by faint blue light had the same energy as those produced by bright blue light.

To explain this, Einstein adopted the idea of quanta that had been proposed by German physicist Max Planck (1858–1947) in 1900 (see box on page 70). Rather than traveling in waves, light could now be thought of as coming in tiny, separate packets. These light quanta would later be known as photons.

Einstein assumed that every quantum of light would carry a specific amount of energy related to the light's frequency. The frequency of light is what determines its color. Blue light has a higher frequency than red and would therefore strike the metal's surface more energetically than red light, and would cause more energetic photons to be emitted. Because all light quanta of the same color have the same frequency and therefore the same energy, increasing the amount of light falling on the metal's surface will not produce more energetic electrons; it will simply produce more quanta to throw off more electrons.

Photons and quanta are more familiar concepts to us today, but they were treated with very deep suspicion by

The Federal Polytechnic School where Einstein studied is now the Swiss Federal Institute of Technology Zurich, also called ETH Zurich.

Here Einstein, Chaim Weizmann, and other leaders of the World Zionist Organization arrive in New York in 1921 on a fund-raising tour.

Einstein's colleagues in 1905. It was only when, in 1916, the processes described by Einstein were experimentally confirmed by American physicist Robert Millikan (1868–1953), who initially had been skeptical of them, that Einstein's views gained wide acceptance. It was for this work that Einstein was awarded the 1921 Nobel Prize in Physics.

MOTION AND THE SPEED OF LIGHT

Einstein developed his ideas further to imagine what it would be like to travel as fast as light. He wrote about them in another of his 1905 papers, "On the Electrodynamics of Moving Bodies," in which he developed what is now known as his special theory of relativity.

The theory concerns movement or motion, and the term "special" arises because it deals with only one special kind of motion, namely what is called uniform motion. This is motion in a straight line at a constant speed, neither getting any faster (accelerating) nor getting any slower (decelerating). In such a case, Einstein insisted, there are no experiments or observations we can make that will let us find out whether we are at rest or in uniform motion. A ball dropped to the floor falls in exactly the same way whether we are on a moving train or standing in the street. We can look out of the train window and see that we are

Passengers on a train moving at constant speed can use the passing trees to see relative motion.

moving by watching the trees flash by. But this is relative motion, and demonstrates only that we are moving relative to the trees, or that the trees are moving relative to the train. If there were no windows and the train moved smoothly at a constant speed, there would be nothing we could do, no matter how sophisticated our instruments, to find out whether we were at rest or in uniform motion. Einstein named this the principle of relativity.

Einstein added as a second principle that the speed of light is constant. That is, wherever and whenever we measure the speed of light, its speed is always the same. This had already been established by James Clerk Maxwell, but because it went against common sense, scientists had tended to dismiss it. After all, reason

seems to suggest that if we are traveling along and shine a flashlight in the direction we are moving, the light will travel at our speed plus the speed of light. If we shine the light in the opposite direction, we expect it to travel at the speed of light minus our speed. Einstein insisted that this is not so: the speed in both cases is the same; it is the speed of light.

Einstein also stated that nothing can move faster than the speed of light, 186,000 miles per second (299,274 km per second). But according to Newton's laws of motion, a force applied to an object causes acceleration (an increase in speed), so in theory it would be possible to accelerate an object indefinitely until it was traveling faster than the speed of light. However, an object's acceleration depends on its mass. The less its mass, the greater its acceleration. Einstein suggested that a force applied to an object provides not only acceleration but also an increase in mass. As the accelerated body approaches the speed of light, its mass increases so dramatically that it would require an infinite force to accelerate it beyond this point. This idea has since been confirmed experimentally by the behavior of electrons in a particle accelerator (a machine for accelerating particles to very high speeds). As they accelerate toward the speed of light, more and more force is required to keep the electrons moving. It may be supposed that this is because as they accelerate they become more massive, and it takes more force to push heavier objects.

ATOMS AND ENERGY

In another of his 1905 papers, Einstein set out one of the most famous formulas in physics, $E = mc^2$. This means that E (energy) equals mass (m) times the square of the speed of light (c). Physicists knew that certain elements emit a flow of energy called radiation when they break down. In 1938 German chemist Otto Hahn (1879–1968) bombarded uranium with neutrons. Hahn found that the uranium split into several products including the lighter element barium (this is called nuclear fission). But the total mass of the barium and everything else that formed was slightly less than that of the original uranium. The "missing" mass had been converted into energy in accordance with Einstein's formula. The amount of energy liberated was tiny. But scientists knew that a single

Particle accelerators, like the one seen here, are often called atom smashers.

Einstein was not directly involved in the US development of the atomic bomb because he did not have the proper security clearance.

gram of uranium contains more than 2.5 x 100,000,000,000,000,000,000,000 atoms. It was clear that just one gram of uranium had the potential to release staggering amounts of energy.

CURVATURE OF SPACE

In his general theory (1915), Einstein considered acceleration. Its central idea, known as the "equivalence principle," states that the inertial mass and gravitational mass of an object are same. Mass can be defined in two ways. Inertial mass is a measure of the extent to which a body resists acceleration when a force is applied to it. The more massive an object is, the greater is the force needed to

accelerate it. If the same force produces in one object twice the acceleration it produces in another object, the second object must have twice the mass of the first. Gravitational mass is produced by gravity, the attractive force between the Earth or other planet and a body in its gravitational field. Suppose a light beam enters through one side of an elevator as it is accelerating uniformly upward, and exits from the opposite side. As the light crosses the elevator, the elevator will have accelerated upward. The path of the light will therefore appear to bend. However, according to the equivalence principle, gravity and uniform acceleration have the same effect on an object because of uniform acceleration. Therefore if light

A SENSE OF RESPONSIBILITY

Einstein had what he termed "a passionate sense of social justice and social responsibility" that stayed with him throughout his life. He was a pacifist (he opposed war) and, after his move to Berlin in 1914, he spoke out against Germany's strong military build-up. But nothing could prevent the inevitable march toward war in Europe. By August that year, World War I had begun. Einstein continued to promote his pacifist views within war-torn Germany. He felt that the whole world was undergoing an "epidemic delusion" that later generations would not understand. However, when the war ended in 1918, Einstein genuinely believed that Germany had renounced militarism, and that the setting up of the League of Nations (the forerunner of the United Nations) to promote peace and international security in 1919 would halt any further aggression.

THE NEW JEWISH STATE

Although Einstein was Jewish, he had not been brought up in a religious home. However, he always insisted that "I am a Jew, and I am glad to belong to the Jewish people...." A growth in anti-Semitism in Berlin after World War I led to his being attacked for his "communist" views, and this worsened when he declared himself a Zionist, a member of the political movement supporting the rights of the Jewish people to establish a national home in Palestine (this aim was achieved in 1948 with the founding of Israel). In 1921 Einstein went with Russian-born chemist and statesman Chaim Weizmann (1874–1952), later first president of Israel, on a fundraising tour of the United States. On the death of Weizmann in 1952, Einstein was invited to become the new president of Israel, but he declined, claiming that he lacked "the natural aptitude and the experience...."

WAR AND PEACE

The 1932 World Disarmament Conference in Geneva was intended to persuade countries to get rid of their weapons. Einstein committed time and great effort to its success, and was distressed when talks broke down. The following year Nazi leader Adolf Hitler (1889–1945) became chancellor of Germany, and the persecution of Jewish citizens began. Einstein left Germany and moved to the United States. In 1939 he wrote a famous letter to President Roosevelt warning of the atomic threat. After the atom bomb was dropped on Hiroshima, Japan, in August 1945, Einstein headed the campaign by scientists protesting its use.

bends, it must also do so because of gravity. So light in a gravitational field will travel in a curved path. However, light takes the shortest path between two points, normally a straight line. If light travels along a curved line, it must mean that the shortest distance is a curved line, and it follows from this that space itself is curved.

According to Einstein's general theory, the curvature of space can be seen as distortions in space produced by the

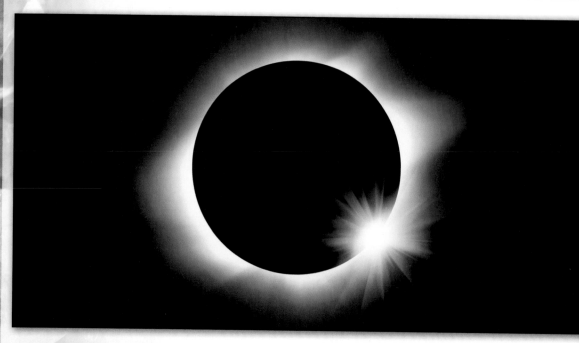

Scientists were able to prove Einstein's predictions during a solar eclipse, like the one seen here.

presence of massive bodies such as the Sun—this is best represented by showing flat space as a rubbery sheet. A planet moving at the right speed and in the right direction as it approaches the Sun would be caught in the dip produced by the Sun's gravitational pull, and then continue to move around it in a curved path, or orbit. The more massive an object, the stronger its gravitational field, because the object creates a greater curvature. Because the distortion is less pronounced at greater distances from the Sun, distant objects are attracted less.

PROOF FROM ABOVE

Was there some way of testing Einstein's claims? As it happened, a total eclipse of the Sun was forecast for 1919, an event that was immediately seen by physicists as a crucial test of the general theory. A total eclipse occurs when the Moon, moving in its orbit around the Earth, comes exactly between the Earth and the Sun. The Moon completely cuts off the light from the Sun so that, as the Earth passes into the Moon's shadow, it is plunged into darkness. Because the Sun is the object with the strongest gravitational field in our solar system, light passing close to the Sun should—according to Einstein's theory—be deflected from its straight-line path, but the Sun emits so much of its own light that any other rays that pass close to it go by unobserved.

However, during a total eclipse the Sun's light is blocked out for a few minutes by the Moon, and for that time other stars are visible during the day. Einstein predicted that the gravitational pull of the Sun would deflect the light of a star by a precise amount, and the star itself would seem to change its position by an equally precise amount. He also predicted that stars in the same direction of the sky as the Sun, but much farther away, would not change their position because they were unaffected by the Sun's gravity.

The eclipse was observed from Sobral in Brazil and from the island of Príncipe, off West Africa, from where it was reported that "the results...gave a definite displacement in good accordance with Einstein's theory." News that Einstein's predictions had been confirmed made headlines around the world. The *New York Times* described the event as "epoch making." Einstein complained that he was so sought after by the press he could "hardly breathe, let alone get down to serious work."

Einstein had to learn to live with the limelight. In later life he became one of the best-known people in the world; with his wild hair and strongly accented English, he came to typify the eccentric scientist in the popular imagination. Books attempted to explain his theories to a nonscientific public.

As a famous figure, Einstein was occasionally able to use his influence in matters of public importance. In 1939 he alerted President Franklin D. Roosevelt (1882–1945) to the dangers of nuclear war.

Nuclear fission had just been achieved by Otto Hahn. A farsighted Hungarian physicist, Leo Szilard (1898–1964), who had emigrated to America as soon as Adolf Hitler came to power in Germany, saw immediately that nuclear fission could lead to the production of weapons of horrendous power. Whatever happened, Nazi Germany must not be the first to get them. Szilard realized that any warning from him would simply be passed around from one office to another and never acted upon.

Einstein was the only scientist who could be sure of being listened to by the U.S. president. Szilard approached Einstein, who immediately agreed to write a warning letter to Roosevelt. It was this initiative that led eventually to the setting up of the Manhattan Project, under which the United States developed the world's first atomic bomb.

PRIVATE LIFE

In 1903 Einstein had married one of his fellow students in Switzerland, Mileva Maric (1875–1948), who was Serbian. Two years previously Maric had become pregnant by Einstein, and she had a daughter, Lieserl, but Einstein never saw the child and nobody knows what happened to her. The couple later had two sons, Hans Albert (1904–1973) and Eduard (1910–1965) but, as Einstein's fame grew and he became increasingly busy, the marriage began to deteriorate. Things were made worse after 1913 when Einstein was made director of physics at the Kaiser Wilhelm Institute in Berlin, and he began to spend much of his time with his cousin Elsa.

Einstein and Mileva separated in 1914, and she returned with their sons to Zurich. In 1916 he asked her for a divorce. When this was granted in 1919

HENDRIK ANTOON LORENTZ 1853–1928

Born in Arnhem in the Netherlands, Hendrik Lorentz studied at Leiden University. In 1875 he wrote a thesis in which he developed James Clerk Maxwell's electromagnetic theory, and in 1878 he became professor of mathematical physics at Leiden University. Lorentz speculated that atoms of matter might be made up of charged particles, and that it is the movement of these that create light. He argued that a magnetic field would affect the movement of the particles, and therefore the wavelength of light. This was proved by his pupil, Pieter Zeeman (1865–1943), in 1896, and is known as the Zeeman Effect. For this discovery the pair were jointly awarded the Nobel Prize in Physics in 1902. In 1904 Lorentz developed the idea that moving objects approaching the speed of light contract in the direction of motion, as also predicted by Einstein's special theory of relativity.

he immediately married Elsa. Mileva was given custody of their two sons. Einstein seems to have had several affairs, but his marriage with Elsa nevertheless lasted until her death in 1936. Einstein was never very close to either of his sons. The younger, Hans Albert, became a hydraulic engineer. The other son, Eduard, suffered a nervous breakdown in the 1930s and was treated with insulin injections and electric shocks. He never really recovered, and for the rest of his life he suffered from the mental disorder schizophrenia. He was looked after by his mother, Mileva, and then, after her death in 1948, by a guardian. In his will Einstein left nothing to his sons. His secretary and his physician were appointed trustees, and he left his estate to the Hebrew University in Jerusalem.

A UNIFIED THEORY

In later years Einstein's work was dominated by two main themes: his opposition to certain interpretations of quantum theory, and his search for a "unified" field theory. It was widely accepted that by the 1930s physicists had developed two successful theories. The first, Einstein's general theory, explained cosmic events in terms of gravity. The second, quantum theory, dealt with the very small, with events at the subatomic level. Einstein tried to find equations that would harmonize the two theories, so that the same framework could be used to explain the behavior of the largest galaxies as well as the smallest subatomic particles. However, he failed to do this, as have all other scientists since, and some people think that pursuing this quest was a waste of much of the latter part of his life.

SCIENTIFIC BACKGROUND

Before 1905

The British physicist James Clerk Maxwell (1831–1879) proposes that light travels in electromagnetic waves

The Dutch physicists Hendrick Lorentz (1853–1926) and Pieter Zeeman (1865–1943) establish that an intense magnetic field affects the wavelengths of light

The American physicists Albert Michelson (1852–1931) and Edward Morley (1838–1923) discover that the speed of light is constant

The German physicist Max Planck (1858–1947) introduces the theory that energy consists of indivisible units (quanta)

1905

1905 Einstein publishes papers on his special theory of relativity, the photoelectric effect, Brownian motion, and the "Equivalence Principle" (that energy is related to mass by the equation $E = mc^2$)

1909 Einstein calls for a theory that will reconcile the fact that light sometimes acts as a wave and sometimes as a particle

1909 Lithuanian mathematician Hermann Minkowski (1864–1909) proposes a four-dimensional model in which space and time are inseparable, paving the way for Einstein's general theory of relativity

1911 Einstein makes the prediction (to be incorporated into his general theory of relativity) that light passing near the Sun will be found to be deflected by the Sun's gravity

1910

1913 The Danish physicist Niels Bohr (1885–1962) proposes a model of the atom in which electrons are arranged in rings around its nucleus

1915

1915 Einstein publishes his general theory of relativity, concerning accelerated motion. One of its predictions is that a redshift will occur if light passes through an intense gravitational field

1919 Einstein's prediction that the gravitational pull of the Sun can bend light is confirmed during a solar eclipse

1920

1921 Einstein wins the Nobel Prize in Physics for his work on the photoelectric effect

1923 Einstein supports work published by the French physicist Louis de Broglie (1892–1987) showing how subatomic particles can be regarded as waves

1922 Einstein's first paper on Unified Field Theory—which is his attempt to explain electric, magnetic, and gravitational forces in terms of each other—is not successful

1925

1926 Inspired by de Broglie's work, the Austrian physicist Erwin Schrödinger (1887–1961) introduces wave mechanics

1925 The gravitational redshift predicted by Einstein is confirmed in astronomical observations

1927 Werner Heisenberg (1901–1976) proposes his Uncertainty Principle: we can never know simultaneously the position and momentum of a subatomic particle

1929 American astronomer Edwin Hubble (1889–1953) establishes that the universe is expanding

1930

1930 Einstein expresses support for the Dutch astronomer Willem de Sitter (1872–1934), who argues that Einstein's general theory of relativity, applied to the universe, favors the idea of an expanding universe

1935

1935 Einstein publishes a paper critical of quantum theory

1938 The German physicist Otto Hahn (1879–1968) splits the uranium atom

After 1940

1942 Italian physicist Enrico Fermi (1901–1954) achieves the first sustained nuclear chain reaction

1953 Einstein presents his final paper, on Unified Field Theory

1965 German-born American astrophysicist Arno Penzias (1933–) and American radioastronomer Robert Wilson (1936–) discover cosmic microwave background radiation, which supports the "hot big bang" theory of the origin of the universe

POLITICAL AND CULTURAL BACKGROUND

1903 Laws to regulate child labor are introduced in the United States

1904 At La Scala opera house in Milan, Italy, the first performance of *Madame Butterfly* by Giacomo Puccini (1858–1924) fails to impress opera critics

1906 Britain launches the battleship *Dreadnaught*, part of an intense naval arms race with Germany and other European powers

1909 The *Jungendherberge* (Youth Hostel) movement is founded in Germany for students on walking tours

1913 The Keystone Picture Corporation signs up British comedian Charlie Chaplin (1889–1977), who will make 35 films in his first year

1914 World War I (1914–18) breaks out in Europe; after rapid advances through Belgium and northern France in August, German forces are halted at the Battle of the Marne, north of Paris

1916 In France, the Germans and French each lose 400,000 dead or wounded in the Battle of Verdun

1918 Summer advances in France exhaust the Germany army, which collapses in the fall. By November World War I is over

1921 Einstein takes part in a fund-raising tour of the United States in support of Zionism (the establishment of a Jewish homeland)

1920 In the United States wartime alcohol restrictions are extended to a complete ban on drinking: Prohibition lasts for 13 years

1925 In Germany, Adolf Hitler (1889–1945) publishes Volume 1 of *Mein Kampf* (My Struggle), his plan to make Germany great by warring against Jews and Communists

1929 Chicago's Mafia gang warfare over control of bootlegging (smuggling) liquor reaches its height with the St. Valentine's Day Massacre, in which seven are killed

1933 With Adolf Hitler about to take power in Germany, Einstein emigrates to the United States; more than 150,000 other Jews will emigrate from Germany

1935 Overcultivation and drought over vast areas of the United States' Great Plains leads to huge dust storms; up to 350,000 people are forced to leave the "Dust Bowl" in search of new homes and work

1936 American author Margaret Mitchell (1900–1949) publishes *Gone with the Wind*, which sells a million copies in six months

1937 American artist and film director Walt Disney completes his first full-length feature film, *Snow White and the Seven Dwarfs*

1941 The United States enters World War II (1939–45) after Japanese planes attack the U.S. Navy base at Pearl Harbor

absolute temperature scale The temperature scale that begins at absolute zero. It is also called the Kelvin temperature scale.

absolute zero The lowest temperature possible (equal to –273°C).

airfoil The cross-sectional shape of an airplane wing, curved more over the top than beneath. Moving through the air, an airfoil produces lift.

amorphous Describing a solid that has no regular shape (it is noncrystalline).

Archimedes' principle The upthrust (buoyant force) on a floating object equals the weight of water it displaces.

atmosphere The layer of gases that surrounds a planet. The Earth's atmosphere is made up of air.

atmospheric pressure The pressure of the Earth's atmosphere at any point on its surface (caused by the weight of the column of air above it). Atmospheric pressure decreases with altitude.

atom The smallest part of a chemical element that can exist on its own. It has a central nucleus (made up of protons and neutrons), surrounded by electrons.

barometer An instrument for measuring atmospheric pressure.

boiling point The temperature at which a liquid changes into a gas or vapor.

bond A link between atoms or ions in a molecule. There are several types, including the covalent bond and the ionic bond.

Boyle's law At constant temperature the pressure of a **gas** is inversely proportional to its volume. For example, if the pressure increases, then the volume decreases.

capillarity Also called capillary action, the movement of a liquid up or down a narrow tube, caused by the attraction between its molecules and those of the tube. The surface of the liquid is curved into a meniscus.

Celsius The temperature scale that has 100 degrees between the freezing point of water (0°C) and the boiling point of water (100°C). It used to be called the centigrade temperature scale.

centigrade The former name for the Celsius temperature scale.

Charles's law The volume of a fixed mass of gas at constant pressure is proportional to its absolute temperature. For example, if the temperature increases, then so does the volume.

compound A substance consisting of molecules formed from the atoms of two or more elements.

compressor A machine for compressing a gas (that is, putting a gas under high pressure).

condensation The process by which a gas or vapor changes into a liquid. The liquid formed is also sometimes called condensation.

condenser An apparatus for converting a gas or vapor into a liquid. (In electronics a device for storing electric charge is also called a condenser.)

covalent bond A type of chemical bond formed between atoms that share one or more electrons.

crystal A solid that has a regular shape because of the ordered way in which its atoms or molecules are arranged.

density For any substance its mass divided by its volume.

drag A force that slows the movement of an object through a fluid (a gas or liquid). It is reduced by streamlining.

ductile Describing a metal that can easily be drawn out to form wire.

elasticity The property of a solid that enables it to return to its original shape after it is stretched (that is, after it has been subjected to stress).

electron A subatomic particle with a negative electric charge. Electrons surround the nucleus of an atom.

element A substance that cannot be broken down in a chemical reaction to form simpler substances. It is also called a chemical element.

evaporation The changing of a liquid into a gas or vapor below its boiling point (caused by molecules escaping from its surface).

Fahrenheit The temperature scale that has 180 degrees between the freezing point of water (32°F) and the boiling point of water (212°F).

fluid A gas or a liquid.

force An influence that changes the shape, position, or movement of an object.

freezing point The temperature at which a liquid changes into a solid. It is the same as the solid's melting point.

friction A force that prevents or slows the movement of one surface against another surface.

gas A state of matter in which the molecules move at random. A gas in a container takes on the size and shape of the container.

Hooke's law The stress on a solid under tension is proportional to the strain.

hydraulic press A machine that uses the pressure of a liquid to "magnify" a force. A small force acting on a small piston produces a much larger force on a larger piston.

ion An electrically charged atom or group of atoms that has either lost one or more electrons (to form a positive ion) or gained one or more electrons (to form a negative ion).

ionic bond A type of chemical bond formed between ions of opposite charge.

Kelvin temperature scale See *absolute temperature scale*.

lift A force acting on a moving airfoil that keeps it in the air (because the lift is greater than the drag).

liquid A state of matter, between a gas and a solid, that has a level surface and, below that surface, takes on the shape of its container.

malleable Describing a metal that can easily be beaten into a thin sheet.

manometer A device for measuring gas pressure, consisting of a U-shaped tube containing a liquid.

mass The amount of matter in an object. See also *weight*.

melting point The temperature at which a solid changes into a liquid. It is the same as the freezing point of the liquid.

meniscus The curved shape of the surface of a liquid in a narrow tube, caused by capillarity.

metal An element (or mixture of elements), usually a hard shiny solid that is a good conductor of heat and electricity.

molecule A combination of at least two atoms that forms the smallest unit of a chemical element or compound.

neutron A subatomic particle with no electric charge that forms part of the nucleus of an atom.

nucleus The central part of an atom, consisting of at least one proton and (usually) one or more neutrons.

pressure The amount of force pressing on a particular area.

proton A subatomic particle with a positive electric charge that forms part of the nucleus of an atom.

salt A chemical compound formed when an acid and a base react. Salt is also the common name for sodium chloride.

solid A state of matter that keeps its own shape (unlike a gas or liquid).

strain The change in shape of a solid object when it is subjected to a stress.

streamlining The shaping of an object so that it presents the least resistance when moving through a fluid (a gas or a liquid).

stress A force that tends to change the shape of a solid object, producing strain.

subatomic particle Any of the various particles that make up atoms. The chief ones are electrons, neutrons, and protons.

superconductor A substance that shows no resistance to the passage of electric current (usually at very low temperatures).

surface tension An effect that makes a liquid appear to have a surface "skin."

turbulence The irregular flow of a fluid moving around an object. It is reduced by streamlining. See also *drag*.

unit cell A group of atoms, ions, or molecules in a crystal that is repeated to form the crystal's three-dimensional structure.

upthrust The apparent loss in weight of a floating object, equal to the buoyant force keeping it afloat. See also *Archimedes' principle*.

vapor Another name for the gas that forms when a liquid boils or evaporates.

viscosity A measure of how easily a liquid flows (that is, how "thick" it is).

weight The force with which a mass is attracted toward the Earth (by the force of gravity).

X-ray A kind of penetrating radiation with a wavelength much shorter than that of light.

American Chemical Society
1155 Sixteenth Street NW
Washington, DC 20036
800-227-5558
Web site: http://www.acs.org
This organization represents profession-
    als of all degree levels who work in
    the field of chemistry and sciences
    that involve chemistry. The ACS pro-
    duces and distributes several
    publications, provides resources for
    students, and assists with profes-
    sional development.

Nagasaki Atomic Bomb Museum
7-8 Hirano-machi
Nagasaki, Japan 852-8117
+81-(0)95-844-1231
Web site: http://www.city.nagasaki.lg.jp/
    peace/english/abm/
On August 9, 1945, the United States
    dropped an atomic bomb on the city
    of Nagasaki, Japan. World War II
    was brought to an end, but the city of
    Nagasaki suffered greatly. This
    museum's exhibits include daily life
    in Nagasaki before the bomb, the
    devastation caused by the blast,
    and an area that encourages
    visitors to consider a world without
    nuclear weapons.

National Atomic Testing Museum
755 E. Flamingo Rd.
Las Vegas, NV 89119
702-794-5151
Web site: http://www.nationalatomictest-
    ingmuseum.org/
This museum, part of the Smithsonian
    Institute, traces the conception,
    development, and testing of the
    atomic bomb. Exhibits on such top-
    ics as radiation and underground
    testing are on permanent display.

National Society of Professional
    Engineers
1420 King St.
Alexandria, VA 22314
703-684-2800
Web site: http://www.nspe.org
This trade organization is made up of
    professional engineers and encour-
    ages members to protect public
    welfare and consider innovative,
    ethica,l and competent practices
    of engineering.

National Weather Service
1325 East West Highway
Silver Spring, MD 20910
Web site: http://www.weather.gov
The division of the US government, part
    of the National Oceanic and
    Atmospheric Administration, pro-
    vides weather, water, and climate
    information, forecasts, and warnings.
    Each year the service collects 76 bil-
    lion observations and provides 1.5
    million weather forecasts and 50,000
    warnings about dangerous conditions.

The National WWII Museum
945 Magazine Street
New Orleans, LA 70130
504-528-1944
Web site: http://www.nationalww2museum.org
This museum, opened in 2000, immerses visitors in America's role in World War II. The museum features several exhibits and artifacts, as well as a 4-D film, *Beyond All Boundaries*.

Nobel Prize
Sturegatan 14
Box 5232 SE-102 45 Stockholm
Sweden
+46 8 663 27 69
Web site: http://www.nobelprize.org
The Nobel Prize is awarded each year in the six categories of Physics, Chemistry, Economic Science, Literature, Physiology or Medicine, and Peace. It is considered one of the most prestigious awards in the world. Winners receive a gold medal, a diploma, and a monetary prize of over $1 million.

Smithsonian National Air and Space Museum
Independence Avenue at 6th Street SW
Washington, DC 20560
202-633-2214
Web site: http://airandspace.si.edu/visit/mall/
This museum showcases the history of air and space exploration and features the Apollo 11 Command Module, the Albert Einstein Planetarium, an observatory open to the public, and much more.

WEB SITES

Due to the changing nature of Internet links, Rosen Publishing has developed an online list of Web sites related to the subject of this book. This site is updated regularly. Please use this link to access the list:

http://www.rosenlinks.com/CORE/Matter

Bethea, Nikole Brooks. *The Water Cycle*. Science Foundations. New York: Chelsea House Publishers, 2012.

Blockley, David. *Bridges: The Science and Art of the World's Most Inspiring Structures*. Oxford, UK: Oxford University Press, 2012.

Burdge, Julia, and Jason Overby. *Chemistry: Atoms First*. New York: McGraw-Hill Science/Engineering/Math, 2011.

Carroll, Sean. *From Eternity to Here: The Quest for the Ultimate Theory of Time*. New York: Plume, 2011.

Carroll, Sean. *The Particle at the End of the Universe: How the Hunt for Higgs Boson Leads Us to the Edge of a New World*. New York: Plume, 2014.

Einstein, Albert. *The World As I See It*. New York: Citadel Press, 2006.

Fetter-Vorm, Jonathan. *Trinity: A Graphic History of the First Atomic Bomb*. New York: Hill & Wang, 2013.

Feynman, Richard P. *QED: the Strange Theory of Light and Matter*. Princeton, NJ: Princeton University Press, 20 06.

Flood, Raymond, Mark McCartney, and Andrew Whitaker. *James Clerk Maxwell: Perspectives on His Life and Work*. Oxford, UK: Oxford University Press, 2014.

Fox, Michael H. *Why We Need Nuclear Power: The Environmental Case*. Oxford, UK: Oxford University Press, 2014.

Gray, Theodore. *The Elements: A Visual Exploration of Every Known Atom in the Universe*. New York: Black Dog and Leventhal Publishers, 2012.

Holmes, Richard. *World War II: The Definitive Visual History*. New York: DK Publishing, 2009.

Isaacson, Walter. *Einstein: His Life and Universe*. New York: Simon & Schuster, 2008.

Maréchal, Yves. *The Hydrogen Bond and the Water Molecule*. Amsterdam: Elsevier Science, 2007.

Rhodes, Richard. *The Making of the Atomic Bomb*. New York: Simon & Schuster, 2013.

Spilsbury, Louise, and Richard Spilsbury. *Atoms and Molecules*. Building Blocks of Matter. Portsmouth, NH: Heinemann, 2007.

Spilsbury, Louise, and Richard Spilsbury. *Solids, Liquids, and Gases*. Essential Physical Science. Portsmouth, NH: Heinemann, 2014.

Symes, R. F., and R. R. Harding. *Crystal and Gem*. New York: DK Publishing, 2008.

Yoder, Claude H. *Ionic Compounds: Applications of Chemistry to Mineralogy*. Hoboken, NJ: Wiley-Interscience, 2007.

PHOTO CREDITS